COMMON BIRDS

OF

QATAR

Hanne & Jens Eriksen

and

Frances Gillespie

Sponsored by

MAERSK
OIL

Privately published by the authors

Acknowledgement

White-throated Robin

The authors owe a great debt of gratitude to Dr Brian Hunter and his wife Louise. An experienced birder, Brian meticulously checked the text, providing essential information local to Qatar. Both he and his wife also gave invaluable assistance with the distribution maps and the histograms.

We also thank Sheikh Faisal Bin Fahad Bin Jassim Al-Thani, Deputy Managing Director, Maersk Oil Qatar AS, for the generous sponsorship by his company which enabled this book to be published.

For enquiries and distribution, please contact:

gillespi@qatar.net.qa *or* hjoman@gmail.com

Text
© *Frances Gillespie*

Photographs
© *Hanne & Jens Eriksen*

Maps
© *Hanne & Jens Eriksen*

Design
Jens Eriksen

ISBN No. 978-9948-15-747-2

Dedication

This book is dedicated to my grandson Jack Ryan, a keen young birder, who is bravely coping with ongoing treatment for leukaemia, and wrote and illustrated a book on Australian birds at the age of eight.

FG

Foreword

The State of Qatar is a relatively small country; an aerial view shows large areas of hamada, the flat desert landscape, bordered in the south by sand dunes and surrounded by shallow seas. Yet this seemingly inhospitable territory is home to a remarkable diversity of fauna, including birdlife. The peninsula's long coastline provides a haven for all kinds of wading birds, from tall flamingoes to the smallest plovers, and twice yearly thousands of birds pass through on migration, some staying a few days, others for several weeks. Other species inhabit Qatar all year round.

Mankind has frequently contributed to the decline and even the extinction of many species, but here in Qatar the reverse is true. Before the oil era the peninsula had no natural surface water and there was little to tempt migrating birds to linger here. Now, the creation of large wetland areas, farms, parks and gardens has vastly increased the number of birds visiting Qatar, and the laws of this country afford them full protection. Almost every year new species are recorded as a 'first' in Qatar.

Bird watchers in Qatar have long felt the need for a simple, easy-to-use field guide to assist with identification of these birds. Having already published several books on Arabian birds, Hanne and Jens Eriksen teamed up with long-term Qatar resident and environmental writer Frances Gillespie, to bring you this book. The contributors would like to thank Maersk Oil, a company committed to protecting Qatar's natural habitat, for their support in helping to bring Common Birds of Qatar *to you.*

Faisal Bin Fahad Bin Jassim Al-Thani
Deputy Managing Director
Maersk Oil, Qatar

Table of Contents

Great Black-headed Gull

Introduction

Why watch birds? There are probably as many answers to this question as there are bird-watchers. But the reasons given have many things in common. Birds are by far the most conspicuous group of animals. They can be studied any time of day (or night), any time of the year and in any place on earth. The bird-watcher can be as young as five or as old as 105 and anything in between. Birds are lively, colourful, have beautiful songs, build intricate nests to raise their families, and migrate huge distances between continents.

Bird-watching can be done alone, or it can be a social event with friends getting together. It can be done on a casual basis, just wanting to know the names of the birds seen on a day at the beach, or one can go out specifically to seek birds in a good bird-watching area. It can also be a lifelong passion, with travels to far-flung places on earth to find all those wonderful species. Bird-watchers may keep a list of birds seen in their gardens or in their country, a list of birds seen in a given year or a life list. It is no wonder then, that bird-watching is one of the fastest-growing hobbies in many parts of the world.

Identifying birds can be an enormous challenge. With some 10,000 species of birds in the world - and 280 species recognized in Qatar - it would be a daunting task to learn them all. Add to this the fact that in many cases male and female birds, young and old, and summer and winter plumages may be different, and one can quickly see the complexity involved in bird identification. No one person has seen all the birds in the world. The world record is about 8,600 species seen.

But bird-watching is first and foremost an enjoyable hobby. To be able to add a name to that flying creature over the coast or in the garden instantly makes it more interesting. We hope with this field guide to be able to help you getting started and add another dimension to your outings in Qatar.

d-watching can be enjoyed by the whole family

About this book

At present, 280 species of birds are named on the Qatar Bird List, excluding around a dozen introduced or escaped species now breeding here. This is an impressive number, considering that a large proportion of the country is desert with no natural surface water and that there are no forests. For the novice bird-watcher, that many species with all the variations in appearance of each species due to sex, age, and time of the year, can make it quite difficult to be confident about an identification. However, of the 280 species, about 65 are very rare and unlikely to be seen. In this guide we have included all species considered common, as well as many species that are not so common but are relatively easy to identify - 215 species in all. So the task of identifying an unfamiliar bird is somewhat reduced.

First, concentrate on the common and conspicuous species and gradually, you will improve your identification skills. Later you may want to tackle the more difficult ones, the 'LBJs' (Little Brown Jobs). You will undoubtedly come across a bird that just doesn't seem to be in the book, and it may not be. Don't worry. Even experts will sometimes have to let a bird pass unidentified. To simplify the task of identification further, we have grouped the species together according to habitat. This has many advantages, but may also lead to pitfalls. If you are in a park or garden in Doha, you should see species like White-eared and Red-vented Bulbul, Laughing Dove, Alexandrine and Rose-ringed Parakeet, House Spar-

Alexandrine Parakeet

row, Indian Silverbill and Common Myna among others. Forget about these species if you are at the coast. On the other hand, the Eurasian Oystercatcher occurs only along the coast. Thus, identifying the habitat cuts down the number of different species to be expected. The trouble is, however, that some birds - like the Laughing Dove - are widespread and may be encountered in more than one habitat. Still, when trying to identify a new bird, start looking in the habitat section of this book that fits best.

We have identified three different habitats: gardens, parks & farmland; the coast & other wetlands; and the desert. Each habitat has been colour coded for easy reference, these being:

Gardens, parks and farms

Lakes, lagoons and coasts

Deserts and arid plains

In Qatar, the locations of the different habitats can be seen in the map to the right. The same colour codes are used at the corner of each page in the main part of this book.

Distribution of birds. When we say a species is common, this is only true in the right habitat and at the right time of the year. For example the Rufous-tailed Shrike can readily be found in parks and farmland from the autumn all through the winter until the spring, but is not here in the summer. Similarly, the Desert Wheatear can commonly be found in winter, mainly in the sandy desert. Resident birds, like the Rose-ringed Parakeet, can of course be seen at any time of year, but in this case only in gardens, parks and farmlands.

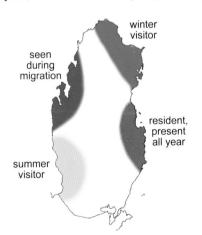

Seasonal occurrence for each bird species in Qatar has been colour coded on the maps as shown to the left.

Size of birds. In the heading for each species of birds is given its approximate length measured from the tip of the bill to the end of the tail. The numbers will be most meaningful when comparing the size of different birds. For example, the Alexandrine Parakeet is a much bigger bird than the Rose-ringed Parakeet.

The status for each species is given as bar diagrams with following code:

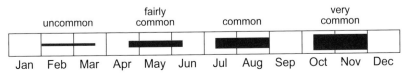

How to watch birds

To get started you need four things: a pair of binoculars, a notebook, a basic field guide (like this one), and a curiosity in the natural world around you. It does not have to be an expensive hobby, even though you could spend a small fortune by adding a telescope, expensive cameras and telephoto lenses or in travelling all over the world in search of new species. However, never forget, you can gain just as much satisfaction and enjoyment by watching and listening out for birds in your own neighbourhood. That is the beauty of birds and bird-watching – anytime, any place, anywhere!

To appreciate birds fully and to learn faster it is best to try to see a bird in as much detail as possible. For this a good pair of binoculars is essential. A notebook is useful for making a list of what you see in a particular area, a good habit to get into. Later, when visiting the same area, a comparison can be made and you will begin to appreciate that some birds may be seen on almost every visit, while others are only seen at a certain time of the year. If you see a bird you cannot identify, try to make a drawing of it, no matter how poor. (Nobody else has to see your artwork!). When you come home you can study the field guide in more detail, perhaps a month or even a year or two later, when, after gaining more experience, you may be able to identify the bird from your drawing and written description.

With so many birds around us, getting started as a bird-watcher may seem bewildering. Try to get familiar with the most common birds first. When you know these you can 'expand' by making comparison with those with which you are by now familiar: 'the new bird seen in November was about the size of a White-eared Bulbul, bigger than a House Sparrow and had a reddish tail and a dark face mask.' This already narrows down the number of possibilities and, in this instance, you will soon be able to work out you have just seen a Rufous-tailed Shrike. Congratulations, that's another new bird for your list!

Binoculars

The only major purchase needed to start bird-watching is a good pair of binoculars. You should expect to pay at least QR 1000 for a decent pair. Cheaper ones are available and may seem adequate at first, but they are probably not dust-proof and within a short time in the field they may be filled with dust and sand, or have moisture on the inside. You could spend a lot more on binoculars, QR 6000 or more, but this is not really necessary at this stage. Later on you may decide to buy the best binoculars, with a lifetime warranty, and if you use them as much as many bird-watchers do it is money well spent (over ten years it works out as less than two riyals per day!).

What should you look for when buying binoculars? Binoculars are rated with two numbers, for example 7 x 35, 8 x 40, 10 x 42 and 10 x 50. The first number is the magnification. You might think the more the better, but magnification greater than 10 times is difficult to hold steady enough for good viewing. The second number is the diameter, in mm, of the big lens in front, the objective lens. The bigger this lens the brighter the view, the image, will be through the binoculars. In Qatar, however, the light is usually so bright you will not need an objective lens much bigger than 40 mm. Also, remember that the bigger the magnification and the bigger the lenses, the heavier the binoculars. This is important as you may need to carry them around your neck for several hours at a time. All in all, the ideal combination of magnification and objective size will be something similar to the numbers mentioned above.

When buying, make sure you test the binoculars yourself, preferably outside the store. Do they feel comfortable in your hands and around your neck? Is the focusing screw easy to reach and operate with your fingers? Is the view through the binoculars clear and sharp all the way to the edges? Are the colours true to life? Some binoculars have yellow coating on the objectives. This may be fine if you want to watch boat races, but no use at all when bird-watching, when appreciating colours can be all important. If you wear glasses, make sure the eye cups on the binoculars can be folded or pushed down so you can get a full view without having to remove your glasses each time.

How to identify birds

Successful bird identification often requires a fair bit of skill from an observer. A bird's plumage and colours are obviously important features, but there are many more. When coming across a new species, perhaps one you have already seen in an unfamiliar plumage, try to work through its features in a systematic way. What is its size in relation to other species of birds you may already know well? Are there any obvious features like a wing bar, a conspicuous eye ring, or brightly-coloured feather tracts? What are the size, shape and colour of its bill, and of its legs? With experience, the call and song of birds become an added help in the identification – and when you are really proficient, if you have heard it first, which is often the case, you may not even need to see most birds to identify them correctly.

As in any new subject there are a few terms that are useful to know in describing a bird. Without going into too much detail, some important ones are illustrated below.

Little Ringed Plover

crown
eye ring
forehead
nape
lore
mantle
bill
back
throat
breast
flank
belly
tail
vent
leg
toe

face mask
iris
upper mandible
supercilium
ear coverts
lower mandible
wing bars

Blue-cheeked Bee-eater

Citrine Wagtail

Wings and tail. In flight, the shape of the wings and tail can give important clues as to the identity of a bird. Large birds of prey, like eagles, have broad wings with almost parallel front and back edges and with some of the primaries showing as 'fingers'. The Eurasian Sparrowhawk has rounded wings, whereas falcons have pointed wings. Gulls have broad wings while terns have narrower, longer wings.

Wing bars can be an important feature. In flight the Common Ringed Plover shows a conspicuous wing bar, but the close relative, the Little Ringed Plover has none.

The shape of the tail and any barring on the tail are also important identification marks. For example, the Swift Tern has a deeply forked tail, while gulls have square-cut tails.

pointed wings

broad wings

Lesser Kestrel

long, narrow tail
with barring

obvious
'fingers'
broad wings
and tail

Eurasian Sparrowhawk

Greater Spotted Eagle

forked tail

broad wings

long, narrow,
pointed wings

Swift Tern

Great Black-headed Gull

Bills. Birds' bills come in all shapes and sizes and give a good indication of the food the birds consume and of their feeding habits. An eagle has a sharp and powerful bill for tearing meat. Sparrows and finches have short, stubby bills indicating they are mainly seed-eaters, while warblers, pipits and wagtails have fine, pointed bills well-suited for eating insects. Waders tend to have long bills for seeking food in the mud. Several species of waders can in fact feed side by side as they differ in bill length, therefore finding food at different depths and avoiding competing with one another for the same worms or other invertebrates. Spoonbills and flamingos have specialized bills and specialized feeding techniques. Spoonbills walk in shallow water, turning the slightly opened bill from side to side and grabbing small food items into the bill. Flamingos and some ducks have what are known as lamellae, not unlike baleen whales. Flocks sieve the water for small organisms by pumping water through the lamellae. Look carefully at the bird's bill every time, it is an important identification feature.

Greater Spotted Eagle
a meat eater

Eurasian Spoonbill
a specialized feeder

Greater Flamingo
a specialized feeder

Eurasian Curlew
feeding on mudflats

Indian Silverbill
a seed eater

Citrine Wagtail
an insect eater

Common Redshank
feeding on mudflats

Legs and feet. The legs of birds are another identification characteristic. Long legs, like those of herons, storks, spoonbills and flamingos, suggest a bird that seeks its food by wading in quite deep water. The powerful legs and claws of the Osprey are useful for catching and holding on to slippery fish - its only diet. Passerines (birds that perch, such as bulbuls and sparrows) have feet that can hold on to a branch even while the bird is asleep. If you see a small passerine on the ground, look carefully how the bird moves. Does it hop like a sparrow or walk like a starling? Terns have small feet and short legs and can barely walk on the beach, although are masters of the air. Ducks have webbed feet and are excellent swimmers. Why not look for tracks in the desert or on mudflats when the tide is out? You will soon learn to identify some birds from their distinctive tracks. This may be the best way to learn if a particular bird is present.

Whiskered Tern
weak legs, no
good for catching
fish

Greater Flamingo
long legs, often
wading in deep water

Indian Silverbill
a passerine or
perching bird

Grey Francolin
strong legs for
running

Mallard
webbed feet for
swimming

Osprey
powerful legs for
catching fish

15

Where to watch birds in Qatar

Although birds can be found almost anywhere in the country, they are not uniformly distributed. To see birds beyond the most common ones you will have to visit several different places at the right time of the year. Here we shall briefly present a few of the good sites in Qatar. If you are a new bird-watcher or do not know any good bird-watching sites in Qatar, the best way to get started is to join one of the tours organized by the Qatar Natural History Group. For details, see More Information on p 21.

Doha area. There are many green places to bird-watch in the city of Doha. Any small area with greenery may hold some interesting birds, especially during migration when anything can turn up. Roundabouts, hotel gardens, golf courses and parks are all worth checking out. At least you should be able to find several common and introduced species such as Laughing Dove, Eurasian Collared Dove, Rose-ringed and Alexandrine Parakeets, Grey Francolin, Common Myna, White-eared and Red-vented Bulbuls and Indian Silverbill. More interesting may be the migrants and winter visitors, amongst them Eurasian Hoopoe, Rufous-tailed Shrike, Black Redstart, Red-rumped Swallow, to mention just a few.

Parkland at the Museum of Islamic Art, Doha

Al Thakhira. About 50 km north of Doha lies an extensive area of tidal mudflats, mangroves and salt-marsh vegetation. This is an important site during migration and in winter for a variety of water birds including herons, ducks, waders, gulls and terns. Eurasian Spoonbill and Greater Flamingo are regularly found. Other noteworthy sightings include Great Cormorant, Western Reef Heron, Western Great Egret, Grey Heron, Mallard, Kentish Plover, Greater Sand Plover, Eurasian Curlew, Common Redshank, Dunlin, Slender-billed Gull and Caspian Tern. It is a favourite destination for resident bird-watchers.

Greater Flamingo

Al Shamal area. At the northern tip of Qatar and a few km east of the town of Madinat Al Shamal lies a mangrove-lined lagoon that is open to the sea. Large wading birds, such as Greater Flamingo, Eurasian Spoonbill and a variety of herons can be found here. At low tide, smaller waders of several species feed in the lagoon and a number of gulls and terns are always present.

Al Shamal area

Man-made wetland at Al Khor

Grey water lagoons. With Qatar's growing quantities of grey water (part of the sewage treatment procedure) lakes and surrounding vegetation have sprung up in several places both near the capital and further afield. No doubt, others will follow as the development of sewage treatment plants continue. The large water bodies attract many different species and some in large numbers. Flocks of ducks, herons, waders, cormorants, gulls and other water birds may be seen. The vegetation and shallow water along the edges will reveal yet other species in search of food. Lots of birding activity can be enjoyed by sitting quietly early morning or late afternoon in the area watching the coming and going of the birds. Unusual species, such as the Purple Swamphen and Eurasian Bittern are essentially found only at these man-made wetland habitas.

Purple Swamphen

Government farm in the interior

Interior Farms. Several government and privately owned farms have been developed in the interior of Qatar. Each farm with its greenery and supply of water attracts a great variety of birds, especially during migration when anything can and does turn up. Rewards may be interesting species such as Common Kestrel, Spanish Sparrow, Eurasian Hoopoe, Namaqua Dove, Rufous-tailed and Blue Rock Thrushes and Eurasian Golden Oriole. Even the much sought-after Hypocolius is a possibility in spring.

Common Kestrel

Ras Abrouq Peninsula. Across from Doha on the west coast lies the peninsula of Ras Abrouq, a favourite camping spot and a good birding area. Long stretches of sandy beaches and low scrub vegetation attract a variety of birds from waders to wheatears. The Hawar Islands, part of the Kingdom of Bahrain, are visible just 3 km offshore. One small island, Suwad Al Janubiyah, is home to a large breeding colony of the Socotra Cormorants which can be seen during the winter months flying along the coastline of Ras Abrouq in long skeins. Ospreys are regular visitors to Ras Abrouq, many of them nesting on the islands. During migration unusual birds have included the Black-eared Wheatear and the splendid White-throated Robin. The Common Ostrich has been introduced on the peninsula, but should not be approached too closely on foot. The male bird can be ill-tempered during the breeding season and give a nasty kick.

White-throated Robin at Ras Abrouq

Osprey

More information

If you are looking for more information on birds and bird-watching in Qatar, check out the website of the Qatar Natural History Group: www.qnhg.org. This is a splendid website giving details of talks and outings. The Qatar Bird Club, established in 2008, which meets at the Friends of the Environment Center, organises bird-watching trips, often led by experienced bird-watchers and wildlife photographers. Joining one of these bird-watching trips is a great way to learn more about birds and get hints on identifying birds. Also check out the links from the website: www.qnhg.org/imp-links. From here there is access to other websites with excellent photos of birds taken within Qatar, and the latest bird sightings. There is also a link to the latest update of the 'Official' Qatar Bird List giving the status of all species currently accepted.

The somewhat outdated *A Birdwatcher's Guide to Qatar* by Christine and John Oldfield (1994) has useful information about birding in Qatar and describes some good sites, although it is no longer reliable as many of the sites have changed. *Important Bird Areas of the Middle East* by M. I. Evans (1994) has a chapter on Qatar, but is also out of date. *Discovering Qatar* by Frances Gillespie (2008) includes up-to-date information on various aspects of the natural history of Qatar and has interesting sections on two special species, the Socotra Cormorant and the Osprey.

For a comprehensive field guide we recommend: *Birds of the Middle East, 2nd ed.* by Richard Porter and Simon Aspinall (Helm Field Guides, 2010). We have generally followed this guide for the English and scientific bird names. Also check out the Ornithological Society of the Middle East (www.osme.org).

Bird-watching can be enjoyed at any age

Bird-watching code of conduct

While bird-watching, it is worth remembering that we are here to enjoy the birds. In our eagerness to get closer to birds to obtain better views we should not forget that the welfare of birds is of top priority. Please adhere to this simple bird-watching 'code of conduct':

- Never harass birds. This is especially true if you are near a nest. Do not alter anything around the nest which might invite a predator as soon as you leave.

- If bird-watching on private land such as farms or date gardens, always ask permission. The landowners are usually happy to have visiting bird-watchers, but simple courtesy tells us to ask first.

- When bird-watching with a group, be sure to move quietly and slowly so as not to disturb birds and ruin the chances for others to see them.

- When out for a picnic or camping trip, please take all rubbish back with you.

- Remember, it is forbidden by law to trap, shoot, kill and harass birds and other living creatures in Qatar.

Happy Birding !

Hanne & Jens Eriksen

Birds of gardens, parks and farms

This is where birdwatching starts. Many of our most common and familiar birds can be found in parks and gardens, even in downtown Doha. If you have access to one of the interior farms or a large garden with trees and lawns you should have plenty of birds around you. Alternatively, visit any of the parks in Doha and birds should be plentiful, especially early in the day.

White-eared Bulbul

Desert Wheatear

White Wagtail

Rose-ringed Parakeet

Other name: Ring-necked Parakeet

Psittacula krameri

40 cm

female

male

This common resident, introduced here, is now well-known in urban areas. Small groups fly screaming across the sky, and hundreds of birds gather at favourite roost sites each evening, where their screeching can be quite deafening.

Despite their noisy behaviour and conspicuous colouring, these parakeets are extremely wary birds and will remain high up in the tallest trees if humans are around. They are not always easy to see from below as their green feathers act as camouflage, but they can always be heard. In flight the long tail is unmistakable. Only the male has the pink and black neck band. They are highly sociable birds and usually fly and feed in groups.

Despite their cautiousness, they will sometimes descend to take fruit from bird tables, and anyone growing sunflowers in their garden will know that Rose-ringed Parakeets find the ripe seeds quite irresistible.

These intelligent birds have been kept as cage pets since ancient Greek and Roman times, and can learn to mimic human speech. They are one of the few parrot species that have adapted well to living in urban habitats, including western Europe.

| Jan | Feb | Mar | Apr | May | Jun | Jul | Aug | Sep | Oct | Nov | Dec |

Alexandrine Parakeet

Psittacula eupatria
55 cm

female

male

Like the previous species, the Alexandrine Parakeet is an introduction to Qatar. It is rather similar in appearance but is larger with a red patch on the shoulder. The bill is much stronger and it has a deeper, hoarser call than the Rose-ringed Parakeet. Only the males have the pink and black neck band. It is much less common than its relative, but numbers in Doha appear to be increasing.

Alexandrine Parakeets often sit on buildings and television aerials and are particularly noisy at sunset when congregating to roost. Their loud calls are often heard long in advance of the birds being seen.

Jan	Feb	Mar	Apr	May	Jun	Jul	Aug	Sep	Oct	Nov	Dec

White-eared Bulbul   *Pycnonotus (leucogenys) leucotis*
Other name: White-cheeked Bulbul   20 cm

Recently split from a very similar Asian species (the Himalayan White-cheeked Bulbul), the White-eared Bulbul is easily recognised by its black head and throat with a large white cheek patch. They are typical friendly garden birds – noisy and conspicuous, and are found wherever there are trees and bushes. This and the following species, both introduced to Qatar from the Indian subcontinent, have spread rapidly and are now common. White-eared Bulbuls also frequent palm groves, farmland and the coastal mangrove forests.

During the breeding season they can become aggressive and squabbling groups of birds will descend from their perches in trees to fight it out on the ground, but the White-eared Bulbul is usually known for its joyful bubbling song and chattering call, sounding like 'come-to-me, come-to-me.' In their search for insects in the crevices of buildings they sometimes catch sight of themselves in windows and will call to their reflections, and they have also been observed doing this when looking in the wing mirrors of cars.

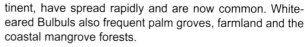

Jan   Feb   Mar   Apr   May   Jun   Jul   Aug   Sep   Oct   Nov   Dec

Red-vented Bulbul

Pycnonotus cafer
20 cm

juvenile

adult

Less common than the preceding species and rather shyer in its behaviour, it is still quite widespread in Qatar in parks and gardens and is a gregarious bird. It is easily identified as the short, stiff crest gives its head a squarish appearance. Usually these bulbuls are dark brown with a white rump and red vent, but occasionally you may see an individual with an orange undertail, a small white cheek spot and black on the breast. This is a hybrid between the White-eared and Red-vented Bulbul.

Jan	Feb	Mar	Apr	May	Jun	Jul	Aug	Sep	Oct	Nov	Dec

Common Myna

Acridotheres tristis
24 cm

Originating in India, the Common Mynas now established in Qatar are probably descendants of escaped cage birds. Over the last three decades they have become abundant in most built-up areas. A large colony roosts in the date palms at one end of the Doha Corniche, and at sunset groups can be seen following each other in looping flight homewards along the sea front, squawking noisily. Some nest in the overhead traffic light gantries along the Corniche and other roads in the city, and despite the roasting heat parent birds can often be seen perched atop the gantries in April/May.

A member of the starling family, Common Mynas are bold and aggressive birds and pose a threat to native species in all the countries where they have been introduced. Like other starlings, when on the ground they walk with a strutting motion rather than hop. In flight the large white wing patches are conspicuous. They are common in gardens, park lawns and on farmland, as well as in urban areas. There is a long-established colony of these gregarious birds at Doha Zoo, attracted by the food available in the enclosures. They are omnivorous, feeding on insects, fruits and discarded human food.

| Jan | Feb | Mar | Apr | May | Jun | Jul | Aug | Sep | Oct | Nov | Dec |

Common Starling

Other name: European Starling

Sturnus vulgaris
20 cm

Despite being referred to as the Common Starling, this species, a winter visitor, is not so common in Qatar. Likely places to find it include grassy fields or reed beds and bushes around wetlands, where it congregates in small, noisy flocks.

In summer the starling has dark plumage with a greenish and purplish metallic sheen. While wintering in Qatar, however, it looks quite different, being all dark with numerous white specks as a result of white feather tips. The sharp, conical bill is black during winter. It is omnivorous, feeding on insects and worms as well as berries and seeds.

| Jan | Feb | Mar | Apr | May | Jun | Jul | Aug | Sep | Oct | Nov | Dec |

House Sparrow

Passer domesticus
15 cm

male

female

House Sparrows are familiar birds throughout Qatar, inhabiting a range of habitats: gardens, cultivations, palm groves, reed beds, desert camps, scrub in semi-desert and even rocky outcrops in the open desert. They can often be seen on the paving and grass along the Doha Corniche.

As their name suggests, House Sparrows are associated with human habitation and the birds often use ledges and roof spaces in inhabited buildings for the sites of their messy nests. They also make nests of large and untidy balls  of grass, often with the odd sweet wrapper or bit of plastic string included, in bushes. Common nesting sites are lintels and roof beams of ruined houses in abandoned villages such as Al Suwaiya near Al Khor, one situated near Lijmiliya in central Qatar and at Al Jemail on the north-west coast. They are social birds, usually occurring in flocks, and are omnivorous, eating seeds and insects but also foraging for waste food left by humans.

At dusk hundreds of birds may settle in one tree, often a date palm, with much noisy chirping before they settle down for the night. They spend a lot of time on the ground and frequently engage in dust baths.

| Jan | Feb | Mar | Apr | May | Jun | Jul | Aug | Sep | Oct | Nov | Dec |

Spanish Sparrow

Passer hispaniolensis
15 cm

male
House Sparrows

male
Spanish Sparrow

Resident breeders in defined colonies, Spanish Sparrows occur in flocks of several hundred on farmlands such as Mukainis and around wetlands, where they nest in trees and shrubs. They can easily be distinguished in spring from their close relatives the House Sparrows by their chestnut brown heads and strong black markings on wings and body, although in winter these colorations are less pronounced. Females are almost indistinguishable from female House Sparrows, and are a muted brown with light streaks on the underparts.

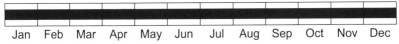

| Jan | Feb | Mar | Apr | May | Jun | Jul | Aug | Sep | Oct | Nov | Dec |

Eurasian Hoopoe

Upupa epops
28 cm

This handsome bird, named *hud-hud* in Arabic, is said in ancient legends to have carried messages between King Solomon and the Queen of Sheba. Its English name echoes its cry: '*hoo-poop-poop*' that can be heard during spring.

A passage migrant, it is unmistakable with its peach-coloured plumage and impressive crest and black-and-white zebra-patterned wings. On sandy ground, where its colours blend into the background, it can look relatively inconspicuous, but in flight the broad black and white wing feathers make an eye-catching display. The crest normally lies flat over the head and is raised only when the bird is excited or alarmed. When disturbed it flies up for a short distance and on landing often raises and lowers its crest.

Hoopoes spend a lot of time on the ground, digging for larvae with their long, slender, curved bills. They can be seen anywhere in Qatar during the migration period – dipping for ants on grassy roundabouts amid swirling city traffic, in parks, on farmland, in oases, around camel camps and far out into the desert on limestone plateaus and in shallow wadis. They are particularly attracted to beetle larvae in cattle and camel dung.

Jan	Feb	Mar	Apr	May	Jun	Jul	Aug	Sep	Oct	Nov	Dec

Laughing Dove

Spilopelia senegalensis
25 cm

The Laughing Dove, sometimes called the Palm Dove, is one of the most common and widespread birds in Qatar. It is found everywhere: parks, gardens, hotel grounds, plantations, towns and villages, around desert camps and in oases, and is invariably associated with human habitation. It can even be seen on seemingly barren parking lots, busily pecking away in the dust. Its diet consists mostly of seeds, with some insects.

These small doves have an annoying habit of staying put on the road as cars approach and then flying up at the last micro-second, but miraculously seem to avoid being hit. Their name comes from their soft, bubbly cooing, usually with 5 syllables: *doo, doo, dooh, dooh, do*, which sounds like laughter. When landing or in flight they sometimes make a high-pitched discordant squeal. They perch on roofs, aerials and telephone wires as well as in trees.

The nest is a flimsy structure of twigs in a tree, or sometimes window ledges or parapets; so minimal is the construction that sometimes they are dislodged by the wind and the eggs or chicks fall to the ground. Males and females look alike, but young birds lack the black spots on the neck.

Jan	Feb	Mar	Apr	May	Jun	Jul	Aug	Sep	Oct	Nov	Dec

Eurasian Collared Dove

Streptopelia decaocto
28 cm

The Eurasian Collared Dove is a common resident throughout Qatar, and is numerous on farmland, where large flocks may occur. It is slightly larger and more heavily built than the Laughing Dove (p 33). Sexes are alike and the black collar on the neck makes it easy to identify. The song is a monotonous repeated 'To-hoo-ho' with the stress on the second syllable. Phonetically, its cooing sounds similar to the Greek word for 'eighteen', *de-caocto*, to which the bird owes its scientific name. Like the Laughing Dove, it sometimes also makes a harsh-sounding call when landing.

It is most often seen in flocks feeding on the ground on farms, and at camel and other livestock camps, and it also frequents the mangrove forests on the northeast coast of the peninsula.

| Jan | Feb | Mar | Apr | May | Jun | Jul | Aug | Sep | Oct | Nov | Dec |

European Turtle Dove

Streptopelia turtur
27 cm

These small, fast-flying doves are fairly common passage migrants in both spring and autumn, and are often found in the company of other doves on farmlands.

The European Turtle Dove is easy to recognise on account of its distinctive black and white neck patch and rufous-edged feathers on the upper wing. The song is a drawn-out, pleasing purr, *'turrrrrr – turrr'* which is quite different from that of the other species of doves in Qatar.

It feeds on the ground and flies off if danger approaches. It often perches with other doves on electrical wires. A careful check through all the birds in a flock of doves may reveal a European Turtle Dove, particularly in the spring.

| Jan | Feb | Mar | Apr | May | Jun | Jul | Aug | Sep | Oct | Nov | Dec |

Namaqua Dove

Oena capensis
28 cm

This charming little dove is becoming more common in Qatar, with several pairs breeding annually. Fortunately it constructs a rather more substantial nest than the other doves, from thin twigs, dried roots and grasses, usually located in a low bush. The two eggs are a creamy yellow.

At first sight it looks deceptively large, but more than half the length of this dove is taken up by its extraordinarily long, thin tail, and the body size is actually very small. Pairs are often seen walking around quietly in search of seeds. The males have striking black markings whereas the female coloration is rather more subdued. The wings show red flight feathers, and the flight is fast and direct.

These doves are not as gregarious as Laughing Doves (p 33), and are usually alone or in pairs, but will congregate in larger numbers where water is available.

Jan	Feb	Mar	Apr	May	Jun	Jul	Aug	Sep	Oct	Nov	Dec

Zebra Dove

Geopelia striata
21 cm

A small resident breeding population of these attractive little doves from southeast Asia is centred around the northern end of the Doha Corniche gardens and in the grounds of the Doha Sheraton. They are most probably descended from escaped cage birds. The birds are slender with a long tail and black and white barring on the brown upperparts. The face is blue-grey with black bars on the side of the neck and pinkish underparts. They forage for seeds and insects on the grass or paving, usually in groups of two or three.

Jan	Feb	Mar	Apr	May	Jun	Jul	Aug	Sep	Oct	Nov	Dec

Indian Silverbill

Other name: White-throated Munia

Lonchura malabarica

11 cm

Indian Silverbills are commonly found on farmlands, wasteland and grassy areas where there is a good supply of grass seed. They also frequent gardens, parks and the rough areas around the edge of the course at the Doha Golf Club.

These small finches generally move around in small flocks, sometimes allowing you to approach closely. On finding grasses with ripe seeds they perch on the grass stems to feed, or hold a stem down with one foot while they strip the seeds. The call is a distinctive, high-pitched, sweet tinkling and, when feeding and moving from tree to tree, a constant soft twittering is heard. Indian Silverbills are sometimes kept as cage birds, and this is probably how they were first introduced into Qatar.

| Jan | Feb | Mar | Apr | May | Jun | Jul | Aug | Sep | Oct | Nov | Dec |

Graceful Prinia

Prinia gracilis
10 cm

A winter visitor and probable regular breeding bird, the small, greyish-brown Graceful Prinia frequents reed beds and tamarisk shrubs around waste water lagoons such as those at Al Khor and Abu Nakhla.

A secretive bird, it is more often heard than seen and hides in dense vegetation much of the time, except in late winter and early spring when it sings from a perch out in the open. The song is a loud, monotonous and continuous '*zeee-tit zeee-tit zeee-tit.*' It is very active, flitting about and frequently cocking its long tail which sways from side to side. Males and females look alike.

| Jan | Feb | Mar | Apr | May | Jun | Jul | Aug | Sep | Oct | Nov | Dec |

European Bee-eater

Merops apiaster
28 cm

Of the two species of bee-eaters regularly visiting Qatar during migration, the European Bee-eater is the most colourful, with almost every colour of the rainbow represented. Both sexes share the same colouring.

This jewel of a bird arrives in late March or early April, having spent the winter in Africa, and their sweet '*croop croop*' calls as they circle in small flocks high in the sky mean that you usually hear them before you see them. They appear as black, delta-winged silhouettes; only when they perch can you see and marvel at their brilliant colours. In Doha and other towns they often fly over swimming pools and gardens in search of their insect prey, perching to take brief rests on aerials, overhead power lines and tree tops. At plantations and farms they circle over the fields looking not only for bees but for any kind of flying insect: grasshoppers, butterflies, dragonflies and flying ants. They remove the stings of bees by repeatedly hitting the insects on a hard surface such as a branch. In open fields they sometimes rest on the ground.

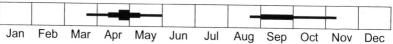

| Jan | Feb | Mar | Apr | May | Jun | Jul | Aug | Sep | Oct | Nov | Dec |

Blue-cheeked Bee-eater

Merops persicus
30 cm

During migration, Blue-cheeked Bee-eaters may be found anywhere in Qatar. They are slightly larger than their relatives the European Bee-eaters, and can easily be distinguished by their emerald-green plumage, yellow chin with chestnut throat patch, and longer central tail-streamers. Though most commonly seen resting on power lines in farmland and plantations they sometimes also roost in tall trees in city parks or hotel gardens. They have also been observed roosting in mangroves and reed beds. The diet of bee-eaters is exclusively insectivorous.

| Jan | Feb | Mar | Apr | May | Jun | Jul | Aug | Sep | Oct | Nov | Dec |

European Roller

Coracias garrulus
30 cm

spring

autumn

The European Roller, a bird of passage, is commonly seen in Qatar only during the spring migration period, late April and early May. It is less common during the autumn migration. At these times the European Roller can turn up almost anywhere, in parks and plantations, and it often frequents sewage treatment plants situated on the outskirts of settlements, where reeds and rough ground are home to its insect and lizard prey.

In spring it is a brilliant bird with its turquoise-blue head and wings and chestnut back. In autumn it can look rather faded and shabby. The colouring of the sexes is similar.

This is a large, powerful and colourful bird with long broad wings showing an iridescent blue patch in flight.

Its favourite food is beetles and grasshoppers but it will also take other insects. The birds sit motionless on wire fences, power lines or tree branches, from which they make sorties to seize their prey on the ground or sometimes in the air.

| Jan | Feb | Mar | Apr | May | Jun | Jul | Aug | Sep | Oct | Nov | Dec |

Eurasian Golden Oriole

Oriolus oriolus
24 cm

juvenile

adult
male

male

The Eurasian Golden Oriole is a fairly common late spring and autumn passage migrant. Good places to look for it include parks and gardens as well as desert oases.

The adult male Eurasian Golden Oriole is a brilliantly yellow and black, thrush-sized bird with a red bill, and cannot be mistaken for any other species. Young males and females that predominate on the autumn passage are olive-yellow in colour. Despite their bright colouring, Eurasian Golden Orioles are shy birds and can be difficult to spot in the dense foliage of a tree. More likely is a glimpse of a large, yellowish bird flying with a fast, undulating flight.

Jan	Feb	Mar	Apr	May	Jun	Jul	Aug	Sep	Oct	Nov	Dec

Grey Francolin

Francolinus pondicerianus
30 cm

The Grey Francolin is an introduced species of partridge. Its overall colour is brown but the back and wings are richly patterned in bars of chestnut, cream and different shades of brown, with darker bars on the breast and belly. The tail is short. They are superbly camouflaged to blend into a dry and sandy environment. These birds have adapted to living in plantations, farms and parks, where they hide among bushes, and can often be seen on the course at the Doha Golf Club.

When approached, Grey Francolins will often wait until the last second and then explode almost from under your feet with a tremendous whirring of wings, flying only a short distance before landing, and they can run swiftly and silently. They prefer running to flying, but even when only half grown the chicks are able to fly.

In the mornings and evenings they make a loud cackling noise – one bird will start up and all the others in the area join in a prolonged chorus. They roost in pairs or in family groups in bushes at night but spend most of their time on the ground during the day, looking mainly for seeds, although they will also eat insects. With their strong bill and feet they scrape away the surface when foraging for food.

Jan	Feb	Mar	Apr	May	Jun	Jul	Aug	Sep	Oct	Nov	Dec

Common Quail

Coturnix coturnix
18 cm

This small bird, a passage migrant, is notoriously difficult to spot, hiding in long grass or crops and creeping away rather than flying. Almost always, the only time you'll see it is when you flush it out at close range, and even then it flies only a short distance before dropping back into cover and crouching low. More often you'll hear its distinctive call, a tri-syllabic whistle *'whit whit-whit'*. It frequents the alfalfa pastures on the inland farms and is often recorded in town gardens on passage.

This little quail is never seen in large numbers. Normally you just come across a single bird. Because of their secretive habits it is very difficult to estimate the numbers visiting Qatar, and many birds will go unnoticed. When seen, they are not hard to identify, looking rather like small, plump pullets. Males and females differ slightly in colouring, with the males having heavier streaking on the face.

Jan	Feb	Mar	Apr	May	Jun	Jul	Aug	Sep	Oct	Nov	Dec

Barn Swallow

Hirundo rustica
19 cm

The Barn Swallow is a common passage migrant, turning up anywhere it can find flying insects, especially over farmlands and irrigated gardens. It sometimes forms large flocks, along with martins (p 48-49).

Birds of the air, Barn Swallows seem to fly endlessly in search of food and only rarely take a rest on electrical wires or other suitable perches. With their dark-blue backs, red throats and streamer-like tails they are easily recognisable and could be confused only with the Red-rumped Swallow. Barn Swallows are most often seen in loose flocks patrolling back and forth over grassy fields. In autumn a good number of birds are juveniles, lacking the typical long tail streamers.

| Jan | Feb | Mar | Apr | May | Jun | Jul | Aug | Sep | Oct | Nov | Dec |

Red-rumped Swallow

Cecropis daurica
18 cm

Much less common than the previous species, the Red-rumped Swallow is sometimes seen in mixed feeding flocks along with Barn Swallows, especially during spring migrations. Likely areas are farmlands and wetlands.

Red-rumped Swallows are relatively easy to pick out in a mixed flock of swallows. It is a relatively heavier bird with apparently slower wing beats. Whereas the Barn Swallow looks all dark above, the Red-rumped Swallow has a pale reddish patch above the base of the tail. If a group of swallows is found on electrical wires, check for birds with a reddish collar and streaking on the breast, which is buff colour rather than the creamy shade of the Barn Swallow's underparts. These will be Red-rumped Swallows. They are never found in Qatar in large numbers, but turn up every year on spring migration.

Jan	Feb	Mar	Apr	May	Jun	Jul	Aug	Sep	Oct	Nov	Dec

47

Sand Martin

Riparia riparia
12 cm

The Sand Martin is a fairly common passage migrant. A small bird, brown above and white below, with a short V-shaped tail, it is much less conspicuous than the Barn Swallow (p 46) and other hirundines with which it sometimes flocks on farmlands and over lagoons as it hunts for airborne insects.

A sandy brown breast band bisects the white underparts and is a good identification clue. To see the band may require some good observation when the birds are flying rapidly over the fields and changing direction all the time, but if resting on a wire the task of identification is easier. Normally encountered in medium to large flocks.

| Jan | Feb | Mar | Apr | May | Jun | Jul | Aug | Sep | Oct | Nov | Dec |

Common House Martin

Delichon urbicum
13 cm

Despite its name, the Common House Martin is the least common hirundine, a passage migrant in Qatar with a few observations in spring extending to summer. It is not numerous, but occasionally turns up in mixed flocks of swallows and martins.

This martin is easy to identify from its glossy blue-black upperparts and striking white rump that can be seen in flight from a considerable distance. No other martin visiting Qatar has a white rump. The underparts are all white. White feathers cover its legs and toes, and the tail is more deeply V-shaped than that of other martins. Like them, it hawks insects by flying endlessly back and forth over grassy areas and other places where flying insects abound. It is less likely than other martins to be seen resting on electrical wires.

| Jan | Feb | Mar | Apr | May | Jun | Jul | Aug | Sep | Oct | Nov | Dec |

Yellow Wagtail

Motacilla flava
17 cm

The Yellow Wagtail is a common passage migrant, seen on farmlands throughout the country, and may turn up in any habitat where insects are found, including the muddy edges of wetlands where it walks busily around on slender black legs with constantly wagging tail.

There are eight races of Yellow Wagtail recorded in the Middle East. In general the Yellow Wagtail has bright yellow underparts and throat and olive-green crown and mantle, with dark greenish-brown primaries on the wings and a dark tail. But head colouring varies and may include black and white, according to the subspecies. Females are browner with a paler yellow/buff below. In Qatar there can be a spring cycle as the different races of European and Asian Yellow Wagtails pass through in sequence heading north.

| Jan | Feb | Mar | Apr | May | Jun | Jul | Aug | Sep | Oct | Nov | Dec |

Citrine Wagtail

Motacilla citreola
17 cm

spring

autumn

The Citrine Wagtail is a regular but uncommon passage migrant and winter visitor, less numerous than the Yellow Wagtail. It is found in the same habitat on farmlands and wet areas.

The Citrine Wagtail closely resembles the Yellow Wagtail except in spring when in its breeding plumage. In autumn and winter look for a yellowish wagtail with a grey back, two clear, white wingbars and a dark patch on the cheek surrounded by yellow. Females are similar in overall markings but with a more washed-out coloration. The Citrine Wagtail is not found in flocks like the Yellow Wagtail. More often it is encountered singly, or just a few birds may be together in areas where there is at least some water present.

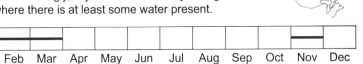

Jan	Feb	Mar	Apr	May	Jun	Jul	Aug	Sep	Oct	Nov	Dec

White Wagtail

Motacilla alba
17 cm

spring

winter

The most numerous and widespread of the wagtails, the White Wagtail is a passage migrant and winter visitor. It can be found in a variety of habitats, from farmlands and parks to wetlands and coastal lagoons. It has adapted to life in busy urban environments, and can be seen picking up ants in car parks. It is commonly seen on the grass plots fringing the Doha Corniche or on the brick paving as it scurries busily around, tail continually wagging.

The White Wagtail is a black, grey and white bird throughout the year. In winter it can look rather dull, but in spring the head pattern is unmistakable, with black throat, crown and nape, and a pure white face surrounding the black, beady eye. Females have more grey and less black.

| Jan | Feb | Mar | Apr | May | Jun | Jul | Aug | Sep | Oct | Nov | Dec |

Grey Wagtail

Motacilla cinerea
18 cm

male

female

The least numerous of the four wagtails seen in Qatar, the Grey Wagtail is a passage migrant and winter visitor. It frequents wetland areas and grassy farmlands.

This bird has a very long tail which is constantly wagging up and down. Whether the bird is foraging or simply resting, the tail is never still. Good identification marks are the grey head with white supercilium, the grey back with black-tipped wings and no obvious wing bars. The underparts are yellow. If disturbed the bird takes off for a short distance in an undulating flight.

Jan	Feb	Mar	Apr	May	Jun	Jul	Aug	Sep	Oct	Nov	Dec

Red-throated Pipit

Anthus cervinus
15 cm

spring

autumn

A passage migrant in spring and autumn, Red-throated Pipits are often seen in flocks on watered lawns.

Slightly smaller and crouching closer to the ground than the Tawny Pipit (p 58) but similar to other pipits in overall appearance, the male and female look much the same. Only in spring does the Red-throated Pipit have a red throat and is then unmistakable. In autumn and winter the bird is heavily streaked on the breast with bold streaking continuing onto the flanks. The mantle is also streaked. This is the most heavily streaked pipit, its markings making it look rather dark from a distance.

| Jan | Feb | Mar | Apr | May | Jun | Jul | Aug | Sep | Oct | Nov | Dec |

Water Pipit

Anthus spinoletta
16 cm

The Water Pipit is a fairly common winter visitor on farm-lands, arriving late in autumn and leaving early in spring.

The Water Pipit is a fairly large, stocky pipit with greyish-brown upperparts, a pale supercilium and a slender bill. The underparts are pale buff with dark streaks. It is the only pipit with black legs. As the name suggests, it favours areas with water: permanent wetlands and grasslands where irrigation leaves standing water on a regular basis. It is not normally seen in large flocks. Individual birds may be seen dashing about trying to catch insects.

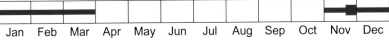

| Jan | Feb | Mar | Apr | May | Jun | Jul | Aug | Sep | Oct | Nov | Dec |

Tree Pipit

Anthus trivialis
15 cm

Passage migrants in small numbers, Tree Pipits may be encountered anywhere there are parks and gardens with trees. They look very similar to Red-throated Pipits and Meadow Pipits, but the streaking is less heavy, especially on the flanks, the bill is heavier and the hind claws shorter. The basic colour of the Tree Pipit is warmer than the other pipits. In autumn, it is an early passage migrant with numbers arriving in September and October before the main arrival of the Red-throated Pipits. Unlike the other pipits, Tree Pipits often perch in trees, but they can also be seen walking on the ground.

Jan	Feb	Mar	Apr	May	Jun	Jul	Aug	Sep	Oct	Nov	Dec

Meadow Pipit

Anthus pratensis
15 cm

Meadow Pipits are scarce winter visitors. Smaller than Tawny Pipits (p 58) and crouching closer to the ground, they are sandy brown above, but are distinguishable from them in that the pale buff breast and underparts are streaked with brown. They can be told from Tree Pipit by less warm colours overall and more heavy streaking on the flanks. The bill is short and thin and the legs are pinkish-brown with long hind claws. Meadow Pipits feed on insects and seeds.

Jan	Feb	Mar	Apr	May	Jun	Jul	Aug	Sep	Oct	Nov	Dec

Tawny Pipit

Anthus campestris
18 cm

A passage migrant and winter visitor, the Tawny Pipit is the most common pipit encountered in Qatar. It is abundant on farmlands.

The Tawny Pipit is a large pipit, often found walking with an upright stance on the open ground in search of insects; it does not sit in trees and bushes. Though many Tawny Pipits can be found on one farm, they are not seen in flocks, instead many individuals will cover a large area. They are undistinguished-looking birds, with sandy brown upperparts. Good identification features for this pipit are the large size, and the lack of conspicuous streaking on the pale underparts.

| Jan | Feb | Mar | Apr | May | Jun | Jul | Aug | Sep | Oct | Nov | Dec |

Spotted Flycatcher

Muscicapa striata
14 cm

Spotted Flycatchers are abundant passage migrants in spring and autumn wherever there are trees and bushes. They perch conspicuously with an upright posture, making short flights to snap up their insect prey. Sometimes an insect eludes them, and then with quick, fluttering twists and turns in the air the pursuit goes on until a meal is secured. They also hunt on the ground for caterpillars. Good identification characteristics of this medium-sized greyish-brown bird include the streaked forehead and faint streaking on the breast.

| Jan | Feb | Mar | Apr | May | Jun | Jul | Aug | Sep | Oct | Nov | Dec |

Red-breasted Flycatcher

Ficedula parva
12 cm

Red-breasted Flycatchers are scarce passage migrants, most often occurring in autumn, and may occasionally be seen where there are trees and bushes. They are small birds. The male is brown with a black tail, edged in white, and pale buff underparts. The robin-like red breast does not develop until the birds are two or three years of age. The pointed bill is black and broad-based, typical of aerial insectivores. These flycatchers will also take insects and caterpillars from the foliage of bushes, and will eat berries if available. They flick their tails as they perch on a high branch, watching out for passing insects.

Jan	Feb	Mar	Apr	May	Jun	Jul	Aug	Sep	Oct	Nov	Dec

Semi-collared Flycatcher
Ficedula semitorquata
13 cm

A scarce passage migrant, the male Semi-collared Fly-catcher is a distinctive small, black and white bird with white breast and underparts. Females, which are less conspicuous, have a brown head, back and wings with white wing-bars. The black bill is broad and pointed. It mainly takes insects in flight rather than hunting for them among bushes or on the ground.

Jan	Feb	Mar	Apr	May	Jun	Jul	Aug	Sep	Oct	Nov	Dec
		▬									

Black Redstart

Phoenicurus ochruros
15 cm

males

female

A common passage migrant and winter visitor, Black Redstarts can be found wherever there are trees where they can perch and launch themselves after airborne or ground insects, and occasionally along the shorelines where they hunt for insects and tiny crustaceans left by the tide.

Some races of Black Redstart wintering in Qatar have extensive rufous underparts. Thus care has to be exercised when identifying Black Redstarts, especially in late spring when Black and Common Redstarts may overlap. Note the greater extent of black on the breast of the male Black Redstart compared to the male Common Redstart. The female Black Redstart is darker than the female Common Redstart. Both species bob up and down and quiver their rufous tails.

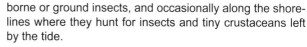

| Jan | Feb | Mar | Apr | May | Jun | Jul | Aug | Sep | Oct | Nov | Dec |

Common Redstart

Phoenicurus phoenicurus

15 cm

female and young male

adult male

Common Redstarts tend not to overwinter in Qatar. The main spring passage of Common Redstarts follows the departure of most Black Redstarts. But care must be exercised from Feb – April when the two species may occur together. Look for the less extensive black on the breast and the white forehead of the male Common Redstart. The habit of both redstarts is the same: they sit quietly on a branch, often in the shade, fly off after an insect and return to the branch, shivering the tail.

Jan	Feb	Mar	Apr	May	Jun	Jul	Aug	Sep	Oct	Nov	Dec

Rufous-tailed Scrub Robin

Other name: Rufous Bush Robin

Cercotrichas galactotes

16 cm

The Rufous-tailed Scrub-Robin is a regular passage migrant in both spring and autumn, with a few birds staying over summer to breed. It may turn up anywhere there are trees or bushes. It is sometimes seen on the edges of grey water lagoons as it hunts among the tamarisk bushes.

This is a conspicuous bird and can often be seen out in the open searching for insects on the ground or under trees. It raises and lowers its rufous tail several times, runs for a bit and repeats the action. While the tail is up, it is often fanned to reveal the dark tip with the white corners. The wings are lowered and sometimes while stopping for a moment the wings are flickered. A black eye-line and a white supercilium complete the obvious identification characters of this species.

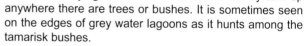

| Jan | Feb | Mar | Apr | May | Jun | Jul | Aug | Sep | Oct | Nov | Dec |

White-throated Robin

Irania gutturalis
17 cm

female

male

An unobtrusive though striking bird, the White-throated Robin is a regular spring passage migrant in Qatar. A little larger than the European Robin, males have dark grey upperparts, a black face with a white supercilium and narrow white throat patch, and bright orange underparts. Females are a lighter greyish-brown with white streaks on the throat and paler orange flanks. Both males and females have black tails. They may be encountered in desert and semi-desert conditions and along the coastline as well as in gardens like those at the Sealine Beach Resort at Mesaieed or the oasis at Ras Abrouq.

Jan	Feb	Mar	Apr	May	Jun	Jul	Aug	Sep	Oct	Nov	Dec

Common Nightingale

Luscinia megarhynchos
16 cm

Thrush Nightingale

Common Nightingale

Common Nightingales are found wherever there are trees and bushes to provide cover, in city gardens and parks as well as in semi-desert areas. The males' sweet, warbling song is rarely heard in Qatar, although migrant birds often utter a few distinctive notes as they feed up to fly on to Europe in spring.

The Common Nightingale is similar in appearance to the much less common **Thrush Nightingale** (*Luscinia luscinia*) that may occasionally be found in similar habitats and at the same time of the year. The Thrush Nightingale is not easily distinguished from the Common Nightingale, but is a slightly darker greyish-brown with mottled markings on the pale buff breast. The tails of both birds are rust-coloured, but the Thrush Nightingale's is a duller shade than that of the Common Nightingale. Both species have pale eye-rings.

Jan Feb Mar Apr May Jun Jul Aug Sep Oct Nov Dec

Desert Wheatear

Oenanthe deserti
15 cm

male

female

A winter visitor, this is the most strikingly coloured of the many species of wheatears regularly found in Qatar. Its wide range of habitats includes farmlands, desert, coastal dunes and even beaches. Oddly, males seem to outnumber females during the winter in Qatar.

The handsome male is distinctive with its black face mask connecting with a broad black patch on the wings when the bird is perched. Unlike all other wheatears the tail has a wide, plain black band up to the level of the uppertail coverts, and this aids in identification. The female resembles an Isabelline Wheatear (p 68), but has more blackish markings on the wing. Both sexes have a distinct white supercilium. It is at home on the ground, but will also perch on low vegetation from where it keeps an eye open for prey on the ground, especially caterpillars.

| Jan | Feb | Mar | Apr | May | Jun | Jul | Aug | Sep | Oct | Nov | Dec |

Isabelline Wheatear

Oenanthe isabellina
16 cm

The Isabelline Wheatear is the most common and widespread passage migrant and winter visitor to farmlands and open, arid country all over Qatar. It is one of the larger wheatears, similar in size to the Northern Wheatear and has a similar upright stance on the ground.

The best field characteristic of this wheatear is the overall uniform greyish-buff colour with only faint black markings on the wings. The lores (areas between the eyes and the bill) are dark. The posture is upright, sleek and elegant. It is often found on the ground, but it may perch on a small rock, a bush or a wire fence to get a better view of the surrounding landscape. It frequently scurries after prey on the ground, and is horizontal when running, but regains its upright stance upon stopping.

| Jan | Feb | Mar | Apr | May | Jun | Jul | Aug | Sep | Oct | Nov | Dec |

Northern Wheatear

Oenanthe oenanthe
15 cm

female

male

A fairly common passage migrant, the Northern Wheatear has a relatively short tail, white with an inverted black 'T'. All wheatears (except the Desert Wheatear, p 67) visiting Qatar have black and white tails; the 'T' of the Northern Wheatear's tail has a wide band at the end and a shorter 'downstroke' than that of the Pied Wheatear (p 70). Males and females have different plumage, the males are handsome birds with a blue-grey back, black mask and wings and white underparts faintly tinged with orange on the throat and upper breast. Females are pale brown above, with brown wings, and buff underparts.

They are active, upright birds, nervous and restless while foraging, bobbing their tails, flicking their wings and making short flights to hawk insects.

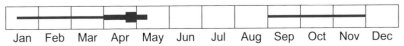

| Jan | Feb | Mar | Apr | May | Jun | Jul | Aug | Sep | Oct | Nov | Dec |

Pied Wheatear

Oenanthe pleschanka
15 cm

female

male

A passage migrant, the Pied Wheatear is a regular visitor to Qatar. In spring the male is white with black throat, wings and back. In autumn they have a black back and bib, a dark crown and buff underparts, fading to white under the tail. Females are brown with buff-coloured heads. These wheatears are relatively long-tailed.

Pied Wheatears prefer open, stony ground at the edge of cultivations. They perch on the top of shrubs or on wire fences, watching for the ground insects on which they feed. They will also eat berries when these are in season.

| Jan | Feb | Mar | Apr | May | Jun | Jul | Aug | Sep | Oct | Nov | Dec |

Eastern Mourning Wheatear

Oenanthe lugens
15 cm

males

Eastern Mourning Wheatears are scarce winter visitors. As the English name implies, these slim and elegant wheatears carry a sooty-black 'mourning cloak' on the back, wings and head of the males. Males have a whitish crown and white underparts with buff under the tail. Females are brown with buff underparts and a blackish bib.

Like other wheatears they perch on isolated trees, wires or fences in open country and semi-desert, making sorties after passing airborne insects or diving to the ground to nab a beetle or larva.

Jan	Feb	Mar	Apr	May	Jun	Jul	Aug	Sep	Oct	Nov	Dec

Black-eared Wheatear

Oenanthe hispanica
15 cm

female

males

The Black-eared Wheatear is an uncommon passage migrant. Males have a black eye-patch extending from the cheek to the bill, black wings, a black and white tail and white underparts, with an ochre tinge colouring the pale mantle and crown. Females are paler with ochre mantle and crown, buff underparts with ochre-coloured breast, and a less vivid dark eye-patch than the male, over which is a pale supercilium.

This wheatear is slimmer and has a longer tail than the Northern Wheatear (p 69), which has a somewhat similar eyepatch and black wings, with more white visible on the spread tail. It spends less time hopping around on the ground in search of insects than the Desert Wheatear (p 67), preferring to perch and then drop down on its prey.

| Jan | Feb | Mar | Apr | May | Jun | Jul | Aug | Sep | Oct | Nov | Dec |

Red-tailed Wheatear

Oenanthe chrysopygia
15 cm

The Red-tailed Wheatear is a common passage migrant and winter visitor, and has been recorded throughout the country anywhere there are isolated rocky outcrops or sparse vegetation. It often perches on a rock, from where it makes short foraging dashes to the ground when an insect or caterpillar is spotted.

While present in Qatar during the winter months, the Red-tailed Wheatear is a rather nondescript bird. The plumage is mostly a brownish grey with a pale throat, and the rump and tail base are a rusty-brown, conspicuous when the bird moves from one perch to another.

Jan	Feb	Mar	Apr	May	Jun	Jul	Aug	Sep	Oct	Nov	Dec

Willow Warbler

Phylloscopus trochilus
11 cm

The Willow Warbler is a fairly common passage migrant in spring and autumn, and can turn up anywhere there are trees and bushes. They are small birds with olive-green backs and wings, pale underparts and a pale, yellowish-tinged breast. The supercilium (the stripe above the eye) is also pale yellow. The Willow Warbler lacks wing bars and its legs are a pinkish colour, unlike those of the Common Chiffchaff which are black.

While in Qatar the Willow Warbler is usually silent. Unlike the Common Chiffchaff, the Willow Warbler often comes to the ground looking for food. Note also that the arrival of the Willow Warbler in spring tends to follow the main departure of the Common Chiffchaff.

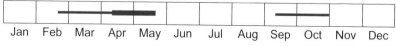

| Jan | Feb | Mar | Apr | May | Jun | Jul | Aug | Sep | Oct | Nov | Dec |

Common Chiffchaff

Phylloscopus collybita
11 cm

The Common Chiffchaff is a common passage migrant and less common winter visitor to areas with trees. It can sometimes be found in the desert where trees occur in gullies among rocks, but is mainly seen in gardens and parks throughout the country.

Great care is needed to separate the Common Chiffchaff from the Willow Warbler. Both are small greenish-coloured warblers. Both are very active looking for food as they flit about in trees and bushes, delicately picking tiny insects from leaves and twigs. The black legs of the Common Chiffchaff are a good field mark. The colouring of the Chiffchaff is duller than that of the Willow Warbler. In late winter and early spring the Common Chiffchaff is occasionally heard in Qatar singing its own name: '*chiff-chaff chiff-chaff*' and identification is straightforward. Chiffchaffs frequently dip the tail when feeding, unlike the Willow Warbler where the movement is less pronounced.

Jan	Feb	Mar	Apr	May	Jun	Jul	Aug	Sep	Oct	Nov	Dec

Common Whitethroat

Sylvia communis
14 cm

The Common Whitethroat is a common passage migrant in spring and autumn. Good places to look for this bird are parks and gardens and also pockets of desert vegetation in oases.

The Common Whitethroat is slightly larger than its close relative the Lesser Whitethroat. Combined with the white throat, the red-brown wing panel (actually rufous edges to the flight feathers) will aid in identification, as will the distinctive orange legs. It darts rapidly among vegetation, flicking its tail. The main diet is insects, but Common Whitethroats will also eat dates if some are left on the palm trees when the birds pass through Qatar on their autumn migration.

| Jan | Feb | Mar | Apr | May | Jun | Jul | Aug | Sep | Oct | Nov | Dec |

Lesser Whitethroat

Sylvia curruca
12 cm

The Lesser Whitethroat is a common passage migrant usually arriving towards the end of the spring migration. It can be found anywhere there are trees and bushes: gardens, parks and oases.

It is a small, greyish warbler with a black ear patch and a pale throat. Spring birds in fresh plumage show a pinkish flush to the lower breast and belly. Obtaining good views may not be easy as the bird often hides in the densest part of the foliage, rarely coming to the ground.

| Jan | Feb | Mar | Apr | May | Jun | Jul | Aug | Sep | Oct | Nov | Dec |

Eastern Olivaceous Warbler

Iduna pallida
13 cm

A regular passage migrant in small numbers, the Eastern Olivaceous Warbler is a pale brown and buff bird with a strong, pointed yellowish bill, not unlike the Clamorous Reed Warbler (p 224) in appearance, but smaller and more attenuated in shape. It prefers semi-open terrain with scattered bushes, or the tamarisk shrubs growing along the banks of the grey water lagoons.

The Eastern Olivaceous Warbler closely resembles its relative the Upcher's Warbler and is very difficult to distinguish in the field.

| Jan | Feb | Mar | Apr | May | Jun | Jul | Aug | Sep | Oct | Nov | Dec |

Upcher's Warbler

Hippolais languida
15 cm

Like the Eastern Olivaceous Warbler, which it resembles, the Upcher's Warbler is a regular spring passage migrant in Qatar in small numbers but is slightly larger, with a longer and darker tail and stronger bill. The eye-stripe is pale. Both birds have an elongated head and bill with a sloping forehead leading to a rounded peak.

The most conspicuous difference between these two birds is the tail movement – Upcher's Warblers slowly wag their tails up and down and from side to side, whereas in Eastern Olivaceous Warblers the tail movement is described as more of an occasional flicking motion.

Jan	Feb	Mar	Apr	May	Jun	Jul	Aug	Sep	Oct	Nov	Dec

Eastern Orphean Warbler

Sylvia crassirostris
16 cm

A scarce passage migrant, the Eastern Orphean Warbler is one of the largest of the warblers. Adult males have a dark grey head with a darker patch on the cheek extending back from the eye, a grey back and a white throat, breast and underparts. Females are brownish-grey with a paler head and buff underparts. A shy bird, it occasionally turns up in areas where there are trees and bushes.

Jan	Feb	Mar	Apr	May	Jun	Jul	Aug	Sep	Oct	Nov	Dec

Ménétriés's Warbler

Sylvia mystacea

13 cm

female

male

A small, active warbler, the male Ménétriés's Warbler has dark ear coverts and forehead, grey head and grey-brown back and wings, and pale underparts with a pinkish tinge on the breast. The eye-ring is yellowish-orange whereas in the female, which is a paler buff colour, the eye-ring is white. The tail with its blackish centre is frequently flicked up and down or from side to side.

Ménétriés's Warblers are passage migrants and winter visitors, seen in Qatar in cultivated areas such as gardens and parks where there are bushes, and in tamarisk bushes around the edges of the wetlands. Like many warblers they feed mainly on insects but will also take berries and seeds.

Jan	Feb	Mar	Apr	May	Jun	Jul	Aug	Sep	Oct	Nov	Dec

Eurasian Blackcap

Sylvia atricapilla
14 cm

female

male

A medium-sized warbler, the male has a slate-grey back and tail and darker grey wings with grey-brown primaries. This passage migrant is well-named for its distinctive black cap. Females are a lighter greyish-brown with a rufous cap. They frequent any area with trees and bushes where they can find their insect prey, and they will also eat berries when available.

Jan	Feb	Mar	Apr	May	Jun	Jul	Aug	Sep	Oct	Nov	Dec

Barred Warbler

Sylvia nisoria
17 cm

immature

adult male

This passage migrant is a large warbler and has distinctive colouring not unlike that of a Common Cuckoo (p 88), with grey head, wings and back and pale undersides barred with dark, crescent-shaped markings. Females are lighter in colour with fainter barrings. The male's rather aggressive-looking eye is yellow or sometimes an orange-yellow. A shy bird, its movements are slower than those of smaller warblers. Like most warblers it is insectivorous but will take berries when they are available.

| Jan | Feb | Mar | Apr | May | Jun | Jul | Aug | Sep | Oct | Nov | Dec |

83

Whinchat

Saxicola rubetra
13 cm

female

male

An occasional passage migrant, the Whinchat is a small bird which often perches on the top of low bushes, from where it makes flycatcher-like sorties after passing insects. It has a prominent white stripe above the eye, with black ear coverts and lores, and is a dark streaky brown on the upperparts and a warm orange-buff on the breast. The bill and legs are black. Females are a lighter brown and lack the black patch on the face, but both sexes have the white supercilium.

Whinchats are rather similar to their close relative the European Stonechats, but are paler and slimmer.

Jan	Feb	Mar	Apr	May	Jun	Jul	Aug	Sep	Oct	Nov	Dec

European Stonechat

Saxicola rubicola
12 cm

European Stonechat
male

male

Siberian Stonechats

female

The European Stonechat is a passage migrant and winter visitor to parks and farmlands throughout the country.

A closely related species, the **Siberian Stonechat** (*Saxicola maurus*), also visit Qatar and the two can be very difficult to tell apart. The male Siberian has a more extensive white collar and less rufous underparts than the European Stonechat. Females of both species are duller with the Siberian female having a pale throat and the European a dark throat.

Stonechats sit conspicuously on a post or in the top of a bush, flicking their wings while on the lookout for insects. If prey is spotted on the ground below, the bird dashes down and returns to the same or a nearby post. Their English name comes from their call, which sounds like two stones being tapped together.

Jan	Feb	Mar	Apr	May	Jun	Jul	Aug	Sep	Oct	Nov	Dec

Common Swift

Apus apus
18 cm

The Common Swift is a passage migrant, rather less frequently seen than its close relative the Pallid Swift. The scientific name comes from a Greek word meaning 'without feet' as these birds are hardly ever seen perching, and even drink, mate and sleep on the wing.

Common Swifts differ from martins and swallows in their very dark plumage and long, narrow, crescent-shaped wings. Unlike swallows these are never folded during the wingstrokes. The underside of the Common Swift is also dark. They are seen over grey water lagoons including Al Khor and Abu Nakhla and also over farmland, in fact anywhere where air-borne insects are plentiful. The flight is extremely fast and agile and swifts often reach great heights while on the wing.

Jan	Feb	Mar	Apr	May	Jun	Jul	Aug	Sep	Oct	Nov	Dec

Pallid Swift

Apus pallidus
17 cm

Pallid Swifts are fairly common passage migrants and winter visitor, seen throughout Qatar and concentrated over grey water lagoons and farmlands. With their long, curved wings and aerodynamic body shape they fly at great speed as they pursue flying insects. Pallid Swifts are more commonly encountered than their relatives the Common Swifts. While silhouetted high against the sky it is hard to tell the two species apart, but in good light the pale throat and lighter grey-brown plumage of the Pallid Swift can be seen.

| Jan | Feb | Mar | Apr | May | Jun | Jul | Aug | Sep | Oct | Nov | Dec |

Common Cuckoo

Cuculus canorus
33 cm

The Common Cuckoo is an occasional passage migrant in both spring and autumn. It may turn up anywhere in Qatar where there are some trees and bushes.

In flight, the long tail, grey upperparts and striped underparts give this bird a resemblance to a Eurasian Sparrowhawk (p 118). It flies fast and straight, again rather like a hawk. It feeds on insects, and is able to eat hairy caterpillars which other birds avoid.

Jan	Feb	Mar	Apr	May	Jun	Jul	Aug	Sep	Oct	Nov	Dec

European Nightjar

Caprimulgus europaeus
26 cm

A fairly common passage migrant, the European Nightjar is not easy to find, due to its secretive behaviour and perfectly camouflaged plumage when sitting on a branch or against the trunk of a tree. They occur wherever there are gardens or parks with trees, and have been seen on lawns fronting multi-storey towers on the Doha Corniche and in the gardens surrounding the Sealine Beach Resort at Mesaieed.

The birds are active at night, with an owl-like, silent, gliding flight. They feed on insects which they scoop up in their enormous gape while flying. The plumage is a mottled lichen-grey and the male has a white spot on each wing, and white spots on the tail, conspicuous during flight. The song is a soft mechanical trilling sound, but is heard only at the breeding ground.

| Jan | Feb | Mar | Apr | May | Jun | Jul | Aug | Sep | Oct | Nov | Dec |

Eurasian Wryneck

Jynx torquilla
18 cm

The Eurasian Wryneck is a passage migrant and is found wherever there are trees. Good places are parks and gardens such as those at the Sealine Resort at Mesaieed or public gardens like those at east coast settlements such as Simaisma and Al Khor.

The Eurasian Wryneck is the only member of the woodpecker family found in Qatar. Its name refers to its ability to turn its head around 180 degrees and its habit of twisting its head rapidly from side to side when alarmed. With its cryptic plumage it can be difficult to spot against the trunk or a branch of a tree. At first sight it could be mistaken for a sparrow or large warbler as it flits unobtrusively among branches, but its shape is more elongated.

Though it likes trees, where it collects ants, it may sometimes be seen foraging on the ground near trees, or at an ants' nest licking up the inhabitants with its sticky tongue. Normally seen singly.

Jan	Feb	Mar	Apr	May	Jun	Jul	Aug	Sep	Oct	Nov	Dec

Barn Owl

Tyto alba
36 cm

A scarce resident breeder, the Barn Owl is unmistakable if seen roosting during the day, with its white, heart-shaped face, ringed with a narrow black line, and black oblique eye-slits. The front is also pale, and the softly shaded reddish-buff and grey wings are beautifully marked. It will roost in old abandoned buildings and also open barns where food sacks are stored that attract its rodent prey.

At night it flies silently, feathered legs dangling, and its very pale coloration makes it easily distinguishable from any other owl.

Jan	Feb	Mar	Apr	May	Jun	Jul	Aug	Sep	Oct	Nov	Dec

Eurasian Scops Owl

Otus scops
20 cm

A passage migrant, the Eurasian Scops Owl could be confused with the Little Owl, but its small ear-tufts are the giveaway; these are lacking on the Little Owl. It is largely nocturnal and if disturbed will fly away for a short distance, its wingbeats alternating with short glides on wings held slightly downwards. However, it is most likely to be encountered sitting motionless at a daytime roost against the trunk of a small tree. Its plumage colour varies from a warm brown to grey-brown, with dark vertical streaks and bars over paler horizontal patches. Its call at night at breeding sites is a clear piping whistle repeated at short intervals, but this is not often heard in Qatar.

Jan	Feb	Mar	Apr	May	Jun	Jul	Aug	Sep	Oct	Nov	Dec

Little Owl

Other name: Lilith Owlet

Athene noctua
23 cm

Little Owls are widespread breeding residents throughout Qatar, nesting under overhanging rock ledges on raised limestone jebel and places such as deserted buildings and walled cemeteries where they are unlikely to be disturbed.

Though they are most active at night, Little Owls can sometimes be seen in late afternoon as they emerge from their daytime hiding roost and sit for a while before setting off hunting. Often a pair or a small family group may be seen together. When alarmed they bob their heads up and down. The pale form *lilith* seen in Qatar is a light creamy brown with pale brown streaks on the plumage of wings and back and a few faint marks on the underparts. The flight is undulating, with wings folded while gliding. The call, heard at night, is a single note: '*keeah*,' repeated at short intervals.

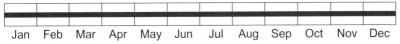

Jan	Feb	Mar	Apr	May	Jun	Jul	Aug	Sep	Oct	Nov	Dec

Red-backed Shrike

Lanius collurio
17 cm

female

male

A strikingly handsome bird, the Red-backed Shrike is a passage migrant most numerous in late spring and easily recognisable with its black 'highwayman's mask', slightly hooked bill, red-brown wings and back and black tail with white edges. Like all shrikes it perches in a prominent position, often on top of a bush or on fencing wires, diving to the ground when prey is spotted. It will eat larger insects such as beetles and grasshoppers and also takes small rodents, reptiles and birds. Shrikes spear surplus food on thorns, barbed-wire or the ends of twigs as a 'larder' against days of bad weather when hunting is limited, hence their nickname 'butcher birds'.

Jan	Feb	Mar	Apr	May	Jun	Jul	Aug	Sep	Oct	Nov	Dec

Rufous-tailed Shrike

Other names: Daurian Shrike, Turkestan Shrike

Lanius isabellinus

17 cm

'Turkestan Shrike'

adults

'Daurian Shrike'

juvenile

Two forms of the Rufous-tailed Shrike visit Qatar: a dark form with strong head markings sometimes referred to as **Turkestan Shrike** and a paler, less well marked form, the **Daurian Shrike**.

The Rufous-tailed Shrike is a common passage migrant and winter visitor all over the country. It is not unlike the Red-backed Shrike in appearance, but is paler with a slightly longer, rusty-red tail. The black facial mask is less clearly defined than on the Red-backed Shrike, and the wings have a white mark visible in flight. It is particularly common during the autumn passage and is found wherever there are trees and bushes. Like other shrikes it has a powerful hooked bill used when tearing its prey apart. If it spots something it swoops down, seizes the prey and returns to the branch to feed.

Jan	Feb	Mar	Apr	May	Jun	Jul	Aug	Sep	Oct	Nov	Dec

Woodchat Shrike

Lanius senator
18 cm

A passage migrant, the Woodchat Shrike is found in open woodlands, parks and farmlands with scattered trees. It is easy to identify from its bold head pattern with extensive, vividly rufous crown and hind neck bordered by black through the eye, combined with white wing panels, throat and underparts. The tail is black, and is not waved up and down while perched as is the tail of the Masked Shrike. Females are similar in pattern but duller in colour. Like other shrikes it perches on the top of a bush, or on wire fencing or electric poles, surveying the ground below for prey. Usually silent while in Qatar.

Jan	Feb	Mar	Apr	May	Jun	Jul	Aug	Sep	Oct	Nov	Dec

Masked Shrike

Lanius nubicus
18 cm

The Masked Shrike is a regular passage migrant, most numerous in spring. It is found in gardens and wooded areas. Despite its name the black 'mask' is less prominent than on other species, for example the Southern Grey or Lesser Grey Shrikes. It is shyer than other species of shrikes and often, when hiding in a bush or sitting on a branch in the shade, it can be hard to see. Once found, it is easy to recognize with its black-and-creamy white plumage and long tail, which it waves up and down when perched. The adult male in breeding plumage has a rufous touch to the flanks.

Jan	Feb	Mar	Apr	May	Jun	Jul	Aug	Sep	Oct	Nov	Dec

Southern Grey Shrike

Lanius meridionalis aucheri
24 cm

The Southern Grey Shrike is a breeding resident and winter visitor over most of the country and found in a wide variety of habitats: parks, woodlands, mountains and deserts. Look for it on farmlands as well as in open, arid areas with some trees. It breeds during the winter months.

This bird can be identified by its grey plumage and extensive black face mask with a narrow, black line above the black hooked bill. It is an aggressive and fearless bird and in addition to its diet of insects, small birds, rodents and lizards it has been known to kill small snakes. Like other shrikes it uses prominent perches from which to swoop on its prey, and spikes surplus food on thorns and twigs as a 'larder'.

| Jan | Feb | Mar | Apr | May | Jun | Jul | Aug | Sep | Oct | Nov | Dec |

Steppe Grey Shrike   *Lanius (meridionalis) pallidirostris*

24 cm

Like the previous species, this is considered by some taxonomists to be a race of *Lanius meridionalis,* but may turn out to be a full species. It is a passage migrant and winter visitor, but much less numerous than the Southern Grey Shrike. Look for it in similar habitats, especially on farmlands.

Skill is needed to identify the Steppe Grey Shrike. It is much paler than the Southern Grey Shrike, has a paler bill, pale lores (areas between the bill and the eyes) and a pale forehead. It is also an aggressive bird that will attack prey almost as big as itself. Like its Southern relative it will impale its prey on a thorn to help it pull the prey apart.

A third species, the Great Grey Shrike, may occasionally be seen in Qatar. It has no black on the forehead and much less white in the wings than the two other species.

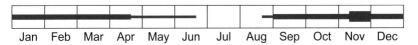

| Jan | Feb | Mar | Apr | May | Jun | Jul | Aug | Sep | Oct | Nov | Dec |

Lesser Grey Shrike

Lanius minor
21 cm

The Lesser Grey Shrike, a passage migrant which normally arrives in Qatar in late April or early May, closely resembles the Southern Grey Shrike but is smaller, with proportionately shorter tail and longer wings. The black 'highwayman's mask' extends above the eye onto the forehead, unlike that of the Southern Grey. The lower breast and belly are often flushed with a pinkish tinge in fresh-plumaged spring birds.

The Lesser Grey Shrike is thought to hoard surplus food by impaling it less often than some of the other species of shrikes. It is typical of shrikes in the region in its diet of larger insects, small reptiles, rodents and birds.

| Jan | Feb | Mar | Apr | May | Jun | Jul | Aug | Sep | Oct | Nov | Dec |

Song Thrush

Turdus philomelos
21 cm

The Song Thrush is a passage migrant and winter visitor, and may turn up in parks and gardens, or anywhere where there is grass and vegetation. It has warm brown upperparts and cream underparts, faintly tinged with buff, on which are conspicuous black spots forming short lines in the direction of the head. Like other thrushes it is omnivorous, eating berries, insects and small reptiles.

Jan	Feb	Mar	Apr	May	Jun	Jul	Aug	Sep	Oct	Nov	Dec

Rufous-tailed Rock Thrush

Monticola saxatilis
19 cm

female

male

The Rufous-tailed Rock Thrush is a regular passage migrant. This medium-sized, stockily-built thrush is mostly seen singly or in small numbers, in rocky areas and in areas of the open desert where there is vegetation.

Males are striking in their appearance, with blue upper-parts, rusty-red underparts and a white patch on the back which is most conspicuous in spring and in flight. Females are brown with pale markings on the upperparts and dark, scaly horizontal bars on the underparts. The tail is rather short and the outer feathers are red in both sexes.

Rufous-tailed Rock Thrushes have an upright stance. They are often seen perched on a rock or on the ground where they hunt for insects and their larvae, and will also take small lizards, and berries when available.

Jan	Feb	Mar	Apr	May	Jun	Jul	Aug	Sep	Oct	Nov	Dec

Blue Rock Thrush

Monticola solitarius
22 cm

female

male

The Blue Rock Thrush is a fairly common passage migrant and rare winter visitor throughout Qatar. True to its name, it is most likely to be seen in areas with some rocks, but may turn up anywhere, including desert oases.

These thrushes have even been seen singing from the corner of a building, which perhaps seems like a rocky landscape to the thrush. They eat insects, berries and small reptiles.

The Blue Rock Thrush is slightly larger than the Rufous-tailed Rock Thrush, with a longer bill. The adult male is a deep slate blue all over. Immature males and females are duller and with more conspicuous bars on the underparts. Compared to the female Rufous-tailed Rock Thrush, the female Blue Rock Thrush is a darker brown and lacks the red tail.

Jan	Feb	Mar	Apr	May	Jun	Jul	Aug	Sep	Oct	Nov	Dec

Crested Lark

Galerida cristata
18 cm

This common lark is a resident breeder and can be found in just about any habitat including open sandy areas within towns and cities, but it is most common in wide open areas such as farmlands and the desert. The Crested Lark is our most common and conspicuous lark. A stocky, round-bellied small bird with a short tail, it is easily identified by the long, spiky crest.

Through much of the year the Crested Lark can be heard, and the soft, fluting song is very pleasing, delivered either from a low bush or in song flight. Male and female look the same and a pair is often seen together on the ground looking for food, mainly insects. The nest is under a bush or tuft of grass on the ground.

| Jan | Feb | Mar | Apr | May | Jun | Jul | Aug | Sep | Oct | Nov | Dec |

Eurasian Skylark

Alauda arvensis
17 cm

The Eurasian Skylark is a scarce winter visitor and much less common than the Crested Lark which is rather similar in size and colouring. It is a streaky brown with a small crest. Although the Eurasian Skylark can raise its crest when excited, most often the crown feathers lie flat over the head. The breast is marked with conspicuous dark stripes, and in flight a white trailing edge to the wings and white sides to the tail are visible. In winter, Eurasian Skylarks favour extensive irrigated green lawns near sewage works, parks and gardens.

While in Qatar Eurasian Skylarks do not sing, but when taking off a call note is heard, something like 'chrrriup', that can be a good identification clue once learned.

Jan	Feb	Mar	Apr	May	Jun	Jul	Aug	Sep	Oct	Nov	Dec

Black-crowned Sparrow-Lark
Other name: Black-crowned Finch Lark

Eremopterix nigriceps
12 cm

female

male

This small bird can be found both on farmlands and in semi-desert. The male is unmistakable with its black and white markings on the head, and its black underparts. The female is quite different, with sandy brown plumage, and looks much like other lark or sparrow species, but can be identified by its small size and the thick bill. Normally, of course, male and females are seen together, both within and outside the breeding season, so identification is rarely a problem. The song is a pleasing, drawn-out whistle of 2-4 notes.

| Jan | Feb | Mar | Apr | May | Jun | Jul | Aug | Sep | Oct | Nov | Dec |

Pale Rockfinch

Other name: Pale Rock Sparrow

Carpospiza brachydactyla

15 cm

A scarce spring passage migrant, this rather drab little bird resembles a female House or Spanish Sparrow (p 30-31), being a sandy-brown on the back and head with darker wings and two paler wingbars. The head has a pale supercilium above the eye and a pale 'moustache' drooping from the bill around the edge of the cheek. It is occasionally seen on farmlands or around areas where there are scattered rocks. It usually forages on the ground and never perches in trees or bushes.

Jan	Feb	Mar	Apr	May	Jun	Jul	Aug	Sep	Oct	Nov	Dec

Ortolan Bunting

Emberiza hortulana
16 cm

female

male

The Ortolan Bunting is a passage migrant, especially in spring. They are normally encountered in small groups on a grassy field, sometimes mixed with other small birds such as pipits, sparrows and other buntings. The birds move slowly through the grass looking for seeds. The male has a greenish-grey head with a yellow eye-ring and a yellow 'moustache' drooping from the bill and bordering the cheeks, which are good identification features. The mantle and wings are brown and the breast is grey; against these the rufous-coloured underparts are conspicuous. Females and young birds generally show the same markings, but are much duller.

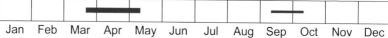

| Jan | Feb | Mar | Apr | May | Jun | Jul | Aug | Sep | Oct | Nov | Dec |

Corn Bunting

Emberiza calandra
17 cm

This rather nondescript, dumpy brown bird is a breeding bird and winter visitor. It is the largest of the buntings and is typically found on open land including grassland, and land where crops have been harvested, where it forages busily for seeds. Characteristically, when disturbed it flutters off with its legs dangling down. The two sexes are similar in plumage, with brown upperparts and streaked buff underparts, but males are about 20% larger than females.

Jan	Feb	Mar	Apr	May	Jun	Jul	Aug	Sep	Oct	Nov	Dec

Little Ringed Plover

Charadrius dubius
30 cm

non-breeding
plumage

breeding
plumage

The Little Ringed Plover is a passage migrant to coasts and inland farmlands where water is available, and grey water lagoons, eating insects and worms. They are more tolerant of humans than other plovers, and in some countries often favour abandoned industrial sites with standing water. A few birds in Qatar stay over summer to breed, nesting in a scrape among stones and relying on camouflage to conceal the eggs.

The Little Ringed Plover is smaller, slimmer and more attenuated in body shape than its close relative the Common Ringed Plover (p 192). In breeding plumage from March to June it is easy to recognize with its bright yellow eye-ring, narrow dark breast-band and white patch above the bill. At other times it looks similar to the Common Ringed Plover, but still has a bit of yellow at the eye and paler legs than that species. In flight, the Little Ringed Plover has no wing bar, unlike the Common Ringed Plover.

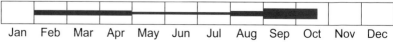

| Jan | Feb | Mar | Apr | May | Jun | Jul | Aug | Sep | Oct | Nov | Dec |

Caspian Plover

Charadrius asiaticus
30 cm

Caspian Plovers visit Qatar mainly on their autumn passage, feeding on insects on grassy farmlands. They are similar to the Greater and Lesser Sand Plovers (pp 190-1) in appearance, with brown upperparts and pale underparts, but have longer legs, and the white supercilium is more pronounced than on either of the sand plovers. The bill is thin and pointed. In winter males and females have a grey-brown breast band.

Jan	Feb	Mar	Apr	May	Jun	Jul	Aug	Sep	Oct	Nov	Dec

Northern Lapwing

Vanellus vanellus
30 cm

An occasional winter visitor, the Northern Lapwing frequents open farmland. This bird is instantly recognisable with its long, wispy, up-turned crest, greenish upperparts and glossy blue wing bands. Younger birds in winter flocks can be rather more subdued in colour with a yellow-brown pattern on the upperparts and a shorter crest. Northern Lapwings are also known as Green Plovers and as Pee-wits; the latter name describes the shrill calls made by the birds.

Northern Lapwings feed on all kinds of small invertebrates.

Jan	Feb	Mar	Apr	May	Jun	Jul	Aug	Sep	Oct	Nov	Dec

White-tailed Lapwing

Vanellus leucurus
28 cm

The White-tailed Lapwing is an occasional passage migrant and winter visitor to Qatar, frequenting open land near water. Adult birds are graceful, slim and erect with a brown back and neck, paler face and greyish-brown breast. The brown wings have a distinctive white and black band along the edge, and the tail is white. These features and its long, bright yellow legs make it easy to recognise. When feeding it tips down steeply with its tail pointing to the sky. In flight the long legs protrude well beyond the tail. White tailed Lapwings occur in ones and twos from about September, but never in large flocks.

| Jan | Feb | Mar | Apr | May | Jun | Jul | Aug | Sep | Oct | Nov | Dec |

Sociable Lapwing

Vanellus gregarius
28 cm

The Sociable Lapwing is a rare autumn passage migrant to farmland in the interior part of Qatar. There are just a few records of this bird here, but this species is included in this book because it is globally endangered, easy to identify and a much sought-after bird. Hence, all records of this bird anywhere are important.

This lapwing looks superficially like the White-tailed Lapwing (p 113), but has a very distinct head pattern with a dark crown and a conspicuous white supercilium. In flight, a striking black and white wing pattern is evident and the white tail has a large, oval-shaped, black spot near the tip.

Sociable Plovers often mix with other lapwings during migration and a flock of eight Sociable Lapwings stayed with 18 Northern Lapwings at Mukainis farm in late autumn 2009. The preferred habitat is a large grassy field where the grass is short so the birds can keep a lookout for any danger.

Jan	Feb	Mar	Apr	May	Jun	Jul	Aug	Sep	Oct	Nov	Dec

Pacific Golden Plover

Pluvialis fulva
24 cm

breeding plumage

non-breeding plumage

The Pacific Golden Plover is a medium-sized plover with long legs and an upright stance. It is a passage migrant and winter visitor to farmlands and coastal areas. During most of the time spent in Qatar Pacific Golden Plovers are in non-breeding plumage, which is rather dull but still has golden markings on the back and on the wings and a yellowish face and breast.

In Qatar records are most common in autumn and early winter. In late April the birds change into their handsome breeding plumage with a broad white line separating the black underparts and the golden highlighted upperparts, but this is not often seen in Qatar.

Food is located mainly by sight rather than probing the ground with the bill; the birds run quickly in an upright position, pausing to peck, then running again. Worldwide, Pacific Golden Plovers have the distinction of flying further than any other bird on their annual migrations except for the Arctic Tern.

Jan	Feb	Mar	Apr	May	Jun	Jul	Aug	Sep	Oct	Nov	Dec

Western Cattle Egret

Bubulcus ibis
50 cm

The Western Cattle Egret is a common passage migrant and winter visitor. It is a small heron that can be distinguished from other white herons (pp 134-6) by its stockier build, short yellow bill, shorter legs and, in spring, some buff-coloured feathers on the crown and breast. It has a short, thick neck and often adopts a hunched posture. The leg colouring varies from yellow in spring to black in autumn.

Western Cattle Egrets are sociable birds, preferring a drier habitat to that of other herons, and large flocks will roam around farms, frequenting the fields where grass or alfalfa is being cut for fodder. They have been recorded in Doha on the lawns and grassy roundabouts along the Corniche in winter, ignoring the roaring traffic as they forage in the grass. Grasshoppers form a major part of their diet, and they will hang around feeding animals on pastureland, or even follow tractors ploughing, hoping to nab insects disturbed by the activity.

Jan	Feb	Mar	Apr	May	Jun	Jul	Aug	Sep	Oct	Nov	Dec

Western White Stork

Ciconia ciconia
100 cm

The Western White Stork is a passage migrant with some birds staying over winter. Small groups of no more than ten may be encountered on farms in the interior of the Qatar peninsula, and they have also been seen in smaller flocks on the north-west coast.

A familiar bird in European folklore, the Western White Stork is easily identified on its black and white plumage and bright red bill and legs. On farmlands these storks walk around grassy fields, favouring areas with newly cut grass, and looking for insects, especially grasshoppers. However, they are omnivorous and will eat anything that turns up: small snakes, toads, fish, rodents and the young of ground-nesting birds. Storks fly with their necks outstretched, unlike the much commoner herons and egrets, and soar and circle slowly before landing. They migrate on hot air currents – 'thermals' – which they use to soar and gain height.

Jan	Feb	Mar	Apr	May	Jun	Jul	Aug	Sep	Oct	Nov	Dec

Eurasian Sparrowhawk

Accipiter nisus
28-38 cm

The Eurasian Sparrowhawk is a scarce winter visitor to Qatar. It's most often encountered in parks and on farmlands, especially where trees are present and crops like alfalfa are grown, such as the privately owned estates at Al Shee-haniya. It is normally seen singly, although more than one may be encountered over a large area.

Usually this hawk is seen by chance as it quarters the air with rapid wingbeats or whizzes low and at high speed over a field in pursuit of its prey, or jinks aerobatically over hedges and trees. It feeds predominantly on small birds up to the size of doves which it normally surprises on the ground and catches as they take flight.

The adult females are rather larger than the males, with a longer tail and lack the reddish-brown cheek and flank colouring of the males. In flight they could be confused with the Common Kestrel (p 122).

Jan	Feb	Mar	Apr	May	Jun	Jul	Aug	Sep	Oct	Nov	Dec

Western Marsh Harrier

Circus aeruginosus
52 cm

male

female

The Western Marsh Harrier, also simply called the Marsh Harrier, is a common passage migrant and winter visitor and is instantly recognisable in flight as a harrier from its wings held slightly up in a shallow V and its long tail. Farmlands in the interior, grey water lagoons with reed beds and the coastal mangrove forests often have one or more Western Marsh Harriers patrolling back and forth for prey. They glide, sometimes with legs dangling and broad wings flapping heavily, just above the reed beds or fields, dropping down from time to time to snatch a toad or small bird. Sometimes they soar high in the air with the primaries splayed out like fingers. They are larger and bulkier than the Pallid Harrier (p 120) and the wings are broader.

The majority of Western Marsh Harriers in Qatar are immature or female birds. They are chocolate brown with a pale, creamy-yellow crown. The front of the wings are sometimes pale. They can be told from other female harriers by the lack of a white rump. Males are much greyer and have a distinctive wing pattern.

Jan	Feb	Mar	Apr	May	Jun	Jul	Aug	Sep	Oct	Nov	Dec

Pallid Harrier

Circus macrourus
40-50 cm

female

male

The Pallid Harrier is a fairly common passage migrant and winter visitor, encountered on fodder fields on farms in the interior and also in coastal areas such as the Ras Abrouq peninsula as it searches for small rodents, lizards and ground-dwelling birds. It is lighter, quicker and more buoyant in flight than the Western Marsh Harrier (p 119). Usually they hunt singly, flying low as they methodically quarter the ground, alternately flapping and gliding with wings held in a shallow V.

Like other harriers, the Pallid Harrier has distinct male and female plumage. The adult male is a handsome bird, very pale grey all over except for a black wedge of primary flight feathers. Immature birds and females are mostly brown with a white rump that is conspicuous in flight. A noticeable feature of the Pallid Harrier is a pale collar behind a darker patch on the cheek.

| Jan | Feb | Mar | Apr | May | Jun | Jul | Aug | Sep | Oct | Nov | Dec |

Montagu's Harrier

Circus pygargus
40-50 cm

females

males

This elegant raptor passes through Qatar mainly on its autumn migration with some individuals over-wintering. Less common than its slightly smaller relative the Pallid Harrier, it is a slim bird with long, pointed wings. Males have grey upperparts and in flight the black wingtips and black wingbars, one above and two below, can be seen. Females are dark brown with paler yellowish-brown underparts and a white rump. They closely resemble the female Pallid Harrier.

Montagu's Harriers have a graceful flight with powerful, fast wingbeats and fly low over the ground in search of prey.

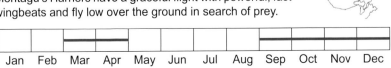

| Jan | Feb | Mar | Apr | May | Jun | Jul | Aug | Sep | Oct | Nov | Dec |

Common Kestrel

Falco tinnunculus
34 cm

female

female

male

male

Common Kestrels are common passage migrants and winter visitors in Qatar. These small falcons are most commonly seen hovering in the capital city, over farm land and in large parks and gardens, where they feed on small birds, small rodents and insects. They often perch on power lines or posts, surveying the ground and watching for the slightest movement indicating prey.

The adult male can be separated from the very similar Lesser Kestrel by its reddish brown upperparts lacking a broad grey line, paler head and a profusion of black spots on the underside. The females of the two species are almost identical. At close range or through binoculars, Common Kestrels can be seen to have black claws while the claws of Lesser Kestrels are white. In addition, Common Kestrels are usually found either singly or as a breeding pair, whereas Lesser Kestrels will sometimes form flocks.

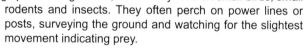

| Jan | Feb | Mar | Apr | May | Jun | Jul | Aug | Sep | Oct | Nov | Dec |

Lesser Kestrel

Falco naumanni
30 cm

female

male

male

female

A globally endangered species, the Lesser Kestrel is a spring and autumn passage migrant and frequents farmlands, preferring grassy fields. Its diet is mainly insects.

Handsome birds, male Lesser Kestrels have blue-grey heads and wing coverts with a rust-red mantle and breast. The breast has vertical rows of darkish spots. Distinguishing this species from Common Kestrels can be tricky. The adult male Lesser Kestrel has darker head, a grey line on the upper wing and fewer black spots on the underside compared with the adult male Common Kestrel. In flight the wings and tail appear shorter than those of Common Kestrels. Females of the two species are reddish-brown with heavily barred wings and mantle, and are virtually identical. The chattering call of the Lesser Kestrel differs from the shrill '*kee-kee-kee*' of the Common Kestrel.

Jan	Feb	Mar	Apr	May	Jun	Jul	Aug	Sep	Oct	Nov	Dec

123

Eurasian Hobby

Falco subbuteo
32 cm

Swifter and more agile on the wing than kestrels, the Eurasian Hobby is a spring and autumn passage migrant through Qatar and is sometimes sighted hunting over farmland. It flies with strong regular wing-beats interspersed with short glides, and its silhouette appears sickle-like. Unlike kestrels, the Eurasian

Hobby does not hover. Such is its speed and skill in flight that it can even snatch swallows and swifts on the wing. It also catches large insects such as dragonflies.

In flight, the long pointed wings and short tail distinguish the Eurasian Hobby from other small falcons. It is slim in build and adults have slate grey upperparts including the tail, with white cheeks and throat and black/dark brown heads. The breast is creamy with lines of dark elongated spots, and the thighs and undertail-coverts a reddish-brown. Females and juveniles are dark brown rather than grey, and juveniles lack the reddish thigh colouring.

Jan	Feb	Mar	Apr	May	Jun	Jul	Aug	Sep	Oct	Nov	Dec

Short-toed Snake Eagle

Circaetus gallicus
65 cm

The Short-toed Snake Eagle is a scarce passage migrant and winter visitor. A medium sized, pale-coloured raptor, it has underwings that in some forms are almost white, in others lightly striped. Other birds are much darker overall. The staring, bright yellow eyes and broad head, flattened on top, give the bird a rather owl-like appearance. It soars with wings held level, sometimes hovering, and the tips of the primary wing feathers held compactly together. At a distance Short-toed Snake Eagles could be mistaken for Ospreys but can be identified by their different flight and broader wings.

Short-toed Snake Eagles hunt over open desert and semi-desert. Their favourite food is snakes but they will also take other reptiles, and small mammals.

| Jan | Feb | Mar | Apr | May | Jun | Jul | Aug | Sep | Oct | Nov | Dec |

Black Kite

Milvus migrans
52 cm

Scarce passage migrants and winter visitors, these buzzard-sized birds have a characteristic forked tail but the indentation is shallower than those of other kites. The plumage is uniformly dark brown with a pale patch sometimes visible on each underwing in immature birds. In flight the Black Kite circles on flat wings, unlike Western Marsh Harriers (p 119) whose wings form a V silhouette.

It is occasionally seen over grey water lagoons, farmland and waste disposal sites. Black Kites have been seen catching fish like an Osprey (p 131), but their diet consists mainly of larger insects such as beetles and grasshoppers, road kill and other carrion.

Jan	Feb	Mar	Apr	May	Jun	Jul	Aug	Sep	Oct	Nov	Dec

Steppe Eagle

Aquila nipalensis
75 cm

An annual winter visitor, the Steppe Eagle is a larger bird than the Greater Spotted Eagle (p 221) but at a distance it can be easy to confuse the two species. When perching the heavily feathered 'trousers' are visible; Greater Spotted Eagles lack these. The upperparts are brown and the flight feathers and tail are a very dark brownish-black, while the underwing coverts are usually paler than the body. The bill has a conspicuous bright yellow gape line extending beyond the eyes. In flight a white line through the centre of the wing is a good identification mark.

Wintering Steppe Eagles tend to favour open areas and cultivated fields in Qatar.

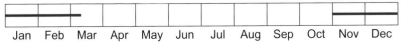

Jan	Feb	Mar	Apr	May	Jun	Jul	Aug	Sep	Oct	Nov	Dec

Hypocolius
Other name: Grey Hypocolius

Hypocolius ampelinus
23 cm

An uncommon, but regular winter visitor, mostly to the west coast of Qatar, the Hypocolius at first sight resembles a Southern Grey Shrike (p 98). It is a slim bird with soft grey plumage, a long tail and a thick, short bill, hooked at the tip. Both males and females have white-tipped black primary wing feathers, but females lack the male's black triangular mask covering the eye.

Hypocoliuses are seen in areas where there are trees or scrub to give them cover, often favouring stands of date palms. They are shy birds and will retreat into thick foliage at any perceived sign of danger, remaining still to avoid detection. Up to half a dozen may occur together, and occasionally they will roost in large flocks. They feed mainly on insects, and also berries and fruit including dates.

Jan	Feb	Mar	Apr	May	Jun	Jul	Aug	Sep	Oct	Nov	Dec

Birds of wetlands and the coast

This section covers birds commonly found at inland lakes, along the coast and around lagoons, in both saline and freshwater habitats. Some species have a preference for one, while most will frequent either. Water birds vary greatly in size ranging from the large Greater Flamingo to the tiny Kentish Plover, and include families like herons, waders, ducks, gulls and terns and other families less well represented.

Greater Flamingo

Bar-tailed Godwit

Greater Flamingo

Phoenicopterus roseus
130 cm

The Greater Flamingo is an abundant winter visitor, mostly to the east coast between Doha and Al Khor but also to the west and north coast of the Qatar peninsula. Recently some birds have taken to staying over the summer. Small flocks are always at Khor al Adaid (the Inland Sea) in the winter months. Some flocks fly inland and can be found on grey water lagoons.

With their pink and white bodies, long gangly legs and odd habit of feeding with their heads upside-down, Greater Flamingoes cannot be mistaken for any other species. In flight their long bodies assume aerodynamic proportions and the flock resembles a long pink ribbon. They feed on minute aquatic invertebrates, plankton and algae by sucking in water and sieving it out through fine lamellae in the beak. Their grunting calls are reminiscent of those of geese, and a flock feeding at night can be heard from a long distance.

| Jan | Feb | Mar | Apr | May | Jun | Jul | Aug | Sep | Oct | Nov | Dec |

Osprey

Pandion haliaetus
60 cm

The Osprey is a local resident, passage migrant and winter visitor. The birds may be found year-round on the Hawar Islands archipelago off the west coast, on islands to the south-east of the Qatar peninsula and on rocky outcrops in the tidal lagoon at Khor al Adaid. They can even be seen in Doha, where for a while a bird used the flagpole in an embassy garden in the West Bay area as a fishing perch.

The Osprey is easy to identify, although in flight it can at first be mistaken for a large gull. The head is pale with a distinctive dark brown stripe through the brilliant yellow eye. The plumage is dark brown above, with pale breast and belly. The diet consists almost exclusively of fish caught by plunging onto the surface of the water, feet first, and locking onto the prey with its talons. Once in the air the fish is manoeuvred to align with the direction of flight to reduce wind resistance and the bird returns to its favourite perch to eat the catch.

| Jan | Feb | Mar | Apr | May | Jun | Jul | Aug | Sep | Oct | Nov | Dec |

Grey Heron

Ardea cinerea
95 cm

The Grey Heron, the largest and commonest of several species of herons in Qatar, is an abundant passage migrant and winter visitor, with many non-breeding birds staying over summer. It is at home on grey water lagoons, where it feeds on frogs as well as fish, mangrove forests, along the Doha and Al Khor Corniches and even in the marinas attached to seaside hotels in Doha. It would

be hard to miss at any of these locations as it stands motionless, watching the water, or slowly stalks its prey.

As the name suggests, these tall birds are mainly grey. Adult birds have black and white markings on the head and neck, with a slender black crest, while young birds are uniformly grey all over. Grey Herons fly with slow, leisurely wing beats and retract their necks into an S-shape during flight, unlike storks and spoonbills which extend their necks. From a distance they can look rather like a large bird of prey, but the semi-circular arch of the wings and the downward pointing tips are a give-away.

| Jan | Feb | Mar | Apr | May | Jun | Jul | Aug | Sep | Oct | Nov | Dec |

Purple Heron

Ardea purpurea
80 cm

The Purple Heron is a passage migrant and winter visitor, with a few non-breeding birds staying over summer. It is most commonly seen at lagoons with reeds that provide some cover, and in mangrove forests.

Seen close to, the reddish colouring that gives this heron its name is visible, but from a distance it looks dark. Many birds seen in Qatar are young birds. Adults have vertical stripes on the long, snake-like neck and a black cap. Whereas the Grey Heron stays out in the open, the Purple Heron prefers to have some cover and can be difficult to spot when it hides in the reed beds. In flight, unlike the Grey Heron, the Purple Heron tends to spread its large feet, giving a less stream-lined appearance.

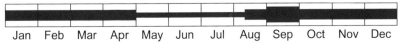

| Jan | Feb | Mar | Apr | May | Jun | Jul | Aug | Sep | Oct | Nov | Dec |

Western Reef Heron

Egretta gularis
60 cm

The Western Reef Heron is an abundant winter visitor to lagoons and open beaches throughout coastal areas of Qatar with many birds found year round.

A medium-sized heron, the Western Reef Heron comes in two main colour forms: a dark grey morph with a white throat and an almost pure white one. There is also an intermediate form. In its white form it can be confused with the Little Egret. The white Western Reef Heron may have a few dark feathers and has a thicker, yellowish bill; Little Egrets have narrow black bills.

Western Reef Herons can sometimes be seen dancing about with half-spread wings and splashing in shallow water. This cunning feeding technique disturbs small fish and the opened wings create a shadowed area on the surface, improving visibility and making it easier for the bird to locate its prey.

| Jan | Feb | Mar | Apr | May | Jun | Jul | Aug | Sep | Oct | Nov | Dec |

Little Egret

Egretta garzetta
60 cm

The Little Egret is a fairly common, non-breeding winter visitor, with a few birds found in Qatar the year round. Its preferred habitat is coastal lagoons and grey water lagoons inland.

Despite its name the Little Egret is a little larger than the Western Cattle Egret (p 116) and is a purer overall white. It can be distinguished by its darker legs and narrow, finely pointed black beak and, in breeding plumage, the long nape plumes. The feet are a greenish-yellow. Immature birds have brownish-green legs and a pink base to the beak. Little Egrets look rather similar to the white form of the Western Reef Heron, but the latter species usually has some green or yellow in the beak and leg colour and the beak is heavier and less sharply pointed.

| Jan | Feb | Mar | Apr | May | Jun | Jul | Aug | Sep | Oct | Nov | Dec |

Western Great Egret

Other name: Great White Egret

Egretta alba
95 cm

The Western Great Egret is a regular passage migrant and winter visitor in small numbers, sometimes seen at tidal mudflats and inland wetlands.

With its large size (the same as a Grey Heron, p 132), pure white plumage, dagger-like yellow bill and black legs, the Western Great Egret is easy to identify. At the lagoons it is conspicuous among other species of herons present, with its long neck often fully extended. In flight the neck is retracted into an S-shape. When feeding in shallow water it is less active than the Little Egret or the Western Reef Heron (pp 134-5), taking a wait-and-see approach to fishing. In spring it develops beautiful white plumes on the back, for which these elegant birds were formerly hunted.

Jan	Feb	Mar	Apr	May	Jun	Jul	Aug	Sep	Oct	Nov	Dec

Squacco Heron

Ardeola ralloides
45 cm

The Squacco Heron is a common passage migrant and winter visitor, frequenting reed beds in grey water lagoons and the coastal mangrove forests. The Abu Nakhla pools are a good place to look for it.

In adult breeding plumage the Squacco Heron is a beautiful bird with golden-buff plumage and long, delicate, chocolate brown and white nape plumes. Juveniles and adults in winter are a camouflaging brownish buff with streaks on the neck and upper breast. In flight both adults and immature birds reveal pure white wings.

Generally solitary in their habits, Squacco Herons will patiently stand and wait for prey, usually among vegetation but occasionally in the open. They often spend the hotter part of the day perched in trees or bushes, coming down to feed at dusk.

| Jan | Feb | Mar | Apr | May | Jun | Jul | Aug | Sep | Oct | Nov | Dec |

137

Striated Heron

Butorides striata
44 cm

adult

juvenile

The Striated Heron is a scarce resident, frequenting mangrove forests, rocky breakwaters, harbours and seawalls on the east coast of the peninsula. This small heron is a skulker and can be quite hard to find. A typical posture is crouched, with head retracted close to the body. Among the mangroves it creeps

slowly through the root system of the trees to emerge at the water's edge where it hunts for small fish, using its powerful bill as a dagger. These herons are said to sometimes make use of 'bait', dropping a leaf, feather or insect lightly onto the surface of the water and nabbing fish that come to investigate.

Adult birds are purplish-grey above, with wing feathers edged with yellow, and a pale grey underside. They have a black cap and yellowish-green legs. Some individuals can be very dark. Juvenile birds are dark brown and stripy all over, similar to but smaller than the Eurasian Bittern (p 141).

Jan	Feb	Mar	Apr	May	Jun	Jul	Aug	Sep	Oct	Nov	Dec

Black-crowned Night Heron

Nycticorax nycticorax
60 cm

adults

juvenile

The Black-crowned Night Heron is a common passage migrant and winter visitor with some non-breeding birds seen over summer. Places to look for this species include reed-fringed lagoons such as the Abu Nakhla pools, where as many as 30 inactive birds may be seen perched together on small trees growing among the thick reeds. They have also been seen near water bodies at the Doha Golf Course.

Black-crowned Night Herons are stockily built, with a pale, soft grey body and wings fading to white on the throat and a black back and crown. Adults in breeding plumage have two or three narrow white 'streamers' extending from the back of the head. Immature birds are striped with spotted brown wings and back. They are most active at night, hence the name, although they can occasionally be seen fishing out in the open during daytime. At dusk they start to move around, and several birds may take to the wing, uttering a distinctive '*quark*.'

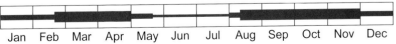

| Jan | Feb | Mar | Apr | May | Jun | Jul | Aug | Sep | Oct | Nov | Dec |

Little Bittern

Ixobrychus minutus
35 cm

juvenile

adult male

The Little Bittern is a fairly common passage migrant and summer visitor to lagoons with reed beds including those at Abu Nakla and Al Khor. Elsewhere, it is scarce.

The smallest of the herons, the Little Bittern is most active in the early morning and at dusk. If alarmed when in the reed beds, Little Bitterns will make themselves as tall as possible, pointing their bill straight upwards and remaining motionless. In this way they look very much like the reeds themselves. If they take to the wing they usually fly only a short distance, with fast wing beats alternating with gliding, before disappearing into the reeds. Adult males are easy to recognize with their black crown and back, females have a black crown, pale buff-coloured breast with striped markings, and dark brown back and wings.

Jan	Feb	Mar	Apr	May	Jun	Jul	Aug	Sep	Oct	Nov	Dec

Eurasian Bittern

Botaurus stellaris
75 cm

This bird requires extensive reed beds in which it skulks, so is seldom seen. Even when in sight its motionless posture and perfectly camouflaged plumage as it stands upright, with extended neck, head and bill aligned with the reeds, makes it very difficult to spot. Eurasian Bitterns are solitary birds, usually only a handful visit Qatar each winter.

Eurasian Bitterns are a species of heron but have thick stocky necks, unlike other herons. The plumage is dark brown with golden streaks and lines of small, arrow-shaped markings. They feed on fish and on the toads which are plentiful at wetlands such as Abu Nakhla, stalking them slowly and then making a sudden stab. At their breeding sites the birds are famous for their extraordinary booming, foghorn-like calls, most often given at night.

Jan	Feb	Mar	Apr	May	Jun	Jul	Aug	Sep	Oct	Nov	Dec

Glossy Ibis

Plegadis falcinellus
60 cm

The Glossy Ibis is a passage migrant and winter visitor to Qatar, staying until May and just possibly, in the case of one or two individuals, over the summer. Its long, down-curved bill makes it easy to identify. From a distance the plumage appears dark brown, but a view through the binoculars reveals beautiful glossy greenish-purplish highlights. Best places to look for Glossy Ibis are the mangrove forests on the east coast and the grey water lagoons inland. In flight it makes a number of rapid wing-beats alternated with long glides, holding its neck outstretched and its legs and feet straight out behind, presenting a stream-lined appearance.

This ibis normally gathers in small flocks but in Qatar the flocks usually number no more than a few birds. Wading in shallow water, it feeds on insects, crustaceans, worms, molluscs, and the occasional small fish, amphibian or reptile.

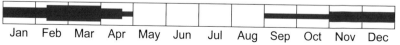

| Jan | Feb | Mar | Apr | May | Jun | Jul | Aug | Sep | Oct | Nov | Dec |

Eurasian Spoonbill

Platalea leucorodia
85 cm

Eurasian Spoonbills are passage migrants and winter visitors, occurring in Qatar only in small numbers. Good places to look for them are the Abu Nakhla lagoons and the mangrove areas around Al Khor on the east coast.

With its white plumage and long, straight, spatula-shaped bill and black legs, the Eurasian Spoonbill is unmistakable. The bill colour varies with the season and with the age of the bird. Adults in spring have a large yellow tip to a black bill and a patch of bare yellow skin on the chin. In winter the bill is all black, while young birds have pinkish-grey bills. When in flight the neck and legs are extended.

Eurasian Spoonbills feed on small fish and aquatic insects, which they sift in side-to-side sweeps of their bills. They can be distinguished from white egrets by their habit of keeping together in small, constantly moving groups.

Jan	Feb	Mar	Apr	May	Jun	Jul	Aug	Sep	Oct	Nov	Dec

143

House Crow

Corvus splendens
42 cm

House Crows are also known as Indian House Crows. In Qatar they are only common on the oil terminal Halul Island, some 90 km NE of Doha. Possibly from the island a few birds have made the flight to the east coast of Qatar and there are now small numbers of localised resident breeders in the area of Al Khor and Ras Laffan.

The birds are slimmer than other corvids, with glossy black plumage on the wings, tail, head, throat and upper breast. The neck and breast are a lighter greyish-brown, and the legs are black.

House Crows are highly gregarious and, as the name suggests, are adapted to living alongside humans. They are aggressive and noisy birds, feeding on human refuse, small birds, eggs and nestlings, rodents, and terrestrial and marine invertebrates.

Jan	Feb	Mar	Apr	May	Jun	Jul	Aug	Sep	Oct	Nov	Dec

144

Great Crested Grebe

Podiceps cristatus
48 cm

breeding plumage

winter

These handsome birds are resident breeders in Qatar, and frequent grey water lagoons and coastal areas. In winter large numbers of grebes including Great Crested and Black-necked Grebes (p 147) have been recorded at sea, some distance from shore, in the shallow seagrass beds between the Ras Abrouq peninsula and the Hawar Islands.

The largest of the grebes in the region, breeding adults are unmistakable with their black crests, chestnut and black ear-coverts and gleaming white fronts. They perform elaborate pairing ceremonies, diving for water weed to offer each other, floating and rearing up breast to breast, and waggling their heads. In winter the plumage is much duller and lacks the crest and colourful ear coverts.

Great Crested Grebes feed mainly on fish and other aquatic animals, but will include crustaceans in their diet. They can be noisy birds in the breeding season, with a variety of harsh grating and chattering calls.

Jan	Feb	Mar	Apr	May	Jun	Jul	Aug	Sep	Oct	Nov	Dec

Little Grebe

Tachybaptus ruficollis
25 cm

juvenile

adult

Little Grebes, also known as Dabchicks, are dumpy little water birds found on most grey water lagoons and open water. They frequent the ponds at the Doha Golf Course and are a breeding bird in Qatar.

A shy bird which prefers the edge of reedbeds and submerged vegetation, the Little Grebe is often heard before it is seen. Listen for the loud, drawn-out trilling call, which has been compared to the whinny of a horse. Normally, the birds hide in dense reeds along the waterside, but when out in the open they can be seen diving for food: insects, molluscs and small fish. Breeding is in the spring and early summer. The young chicks have black and white stripes on the head, and sometimes hitch a ride on a parent's back with just their heads peeping out from under the wings.

Jan	Feb	Mar	Apr	May	Jun	Jul	Aug	Sep	Oct	Nov	Dec

Black-necked Grebe

Podiceps nigricollis
30 cm

breeding plumage

winter

The Black-necked Grebe is a common passage migrant and winter visitor to grey water lagoons and coastal areas, including the Ras Abrouq peninsula. This grebe is more often seen in open water and does not skulk in reed beds as does the Little Grebe. It dives and dabbles for aquatic insects.

The steeply sloping forehead, short bill and triangular head-shape give it a characteristic profile, and the large, bright red eye is conspicuous. In winter plumage its white throat and cheeks contrast with a grey neck and black and grey body. Sometimes a little flock of birds may be seen floating together, then suddenly they all dive and disappear for a moment. Most birds in Qatar will be seen in winter plumage, but in spring the birds take on a beautiful breeding plumage.

Jan	Feb	Mar	Apr	May	Jun	Jul	Aug	Sep	Oct	Nov	Dec

Great Cormorant

Phalacrocorax carbo
90 cm

breeding plumage

winter

Great Cormorants are large, black fish-eating birds found along rocky coastlines, grey water lagoons and also around harbours. They are similar in appearance to the related species, the Socotra Cormorant, but can be told apart because the Great Cormorant is the bigger of the two and has some bare yellow skin at the chin. They can be seen perching on buoys and jetties around Doha's marinas, often with wings spread, and some birds may fly inland to spend the night on one of the grey water lagoons. They fly in long undulating lines or loose V formations often seen at dusk over Doha.

The breeding plumage is attained in March and consists of extensive white markings on the head and upper neck and a large white spot on the thigh.

| Jan | Feb | Mar | Apr | May | Jun | Jul | Aug | Sep | Oct | Nov | Dec |

Socotra Cormorant

Phalacrocorax nigrogularis
80 cm

The adult Socotra Cormorant is black all over with a pale bill. It has a finer bill and is more slimly proportioned than its larger relative, the Great Cormorant, and has no white markings on the head. Immature birds are brownish grey, often with extensive pale markings on the lower breast and belly.

Up to 25,000 pairs nest each year on Suwad al Janubiyah, one of the Hawar Islands archipelago off the west coast of Qatar. In winter huge flocks numbering thousands of birds can be seen offshore flying along the northern coasts of Qatar. Intensely social birds, when fishing they alight on the sea in great flocks which move forward in a rolling motion, the rear end of the flock continually leapfrogging to the front.

Jan	Feb	Mar	Apr	May	Jun	Jul	Aug	Sep	Oct	Nov	Dec

Mallard

Anas platyrhynchos
55 cm

duck

drake

The Mallard is a common winter visitor to grey water lagoons and coastal regions. It also frequents the ponds at the Doha Golf Club. This familiar duck is easy to identify as far as the drake in breeding plumage is concerned. The head is an iridescent green, and can look almost purple from some angles. At the rear end are two smart, up-curled feathers. Females are darker brown overall. A brightly coloured, blue/green wing patch called the speculum is present in both the male and female and is bordered by a white line. It is usually kept hidden in the folded wing when the birds are swimming or walking, but becomes conspicuous when the birds are in flight.

Mallards will often forage quite far from water. Male Mallards are rather silent compared with females but sometimes utter a nasal call; it is the female which makes the well-known quacking.

Jan	Feb	Mar	Apr	May	Jun	Jul	Aug	Sep	Oct	Nov	Dec

150

Gadwall

Anas strepera
50 cm

drake
non-breeding plumage
resembling female

drake
breeding plumage

The Gadwall, a medium-sized dabbling duck, is a fairly common winter visitor. Compared to other male ducks the drake Gadwall is more sombre in colour, basically dark grey with a black rump. Females are a chestnut-brown with darker-brown V-shaped markings. The best field mark is the white speculum (a patch on the wing). Gadwalls tend to swim high in the water with their rear end elevated, so the white wing patch is visible. The patch is conspicuous in flight in both male and female. The female's bill is reddish-orange in colour whereas the male's is dark with an orange undertinge near the base.

Gadwalls fly with rapid wing beats and pointed wings. Numbers seen together are not usually large, and a flock of up to ten might be found in Qatar.

Jan	Feb	Mar	Apr	May	Jun	Jul	Aug	Sep	Oct	Nov	Dec

151

Northern Pintail

Anas acuta
55 cm

duck

drake

The Northern Pintail is a relatively abundant passage migrant and winter visitor mostly found at grey water lagoons and coastal areas.

Northern Pintails have long necks, rounded heads and dark, narrow bills. Their English and scientific names derive from the long, pointed tail feathers present in both the duck and the drake. The long neck and the long tail give the bird a rather elegant appearance. The drake is a handsome bird with the vertical, white line on the neck, grey body and conspicuous pale patches on the side of the rump. The female is uniformly brown and paler than other female ducks. In flight the long neck and pointed tail are good field marks.

Pintails dabble for plant food and will also take small invertebrates.

| Jan | Feb | Mar | Apr | May | Jun | Jul | Aug | Sep | Oct | Nov | Dec |

Northern Shoveler

Anas clypeata
50 cm

ducks

drake

The Northern Shoveler, a relatively common winter visitor to lakes, shorelines and coastal lagoons, is a heavy-looking duck. Its name is derived from its large spatulate bill. Both female and male (duck and drake) have this oversized bill and the birds can be identified on the bill alone. The drakes are colourful birds with their green head, white breast and chestnut-brown belly and flanks. In flight, pale blue forewing feathers are separated from the green speculum (wing patch) by a narrow white border. The females, like other female ducks, are plain-looking and brown with grey forewings.

Northern Shovelers look front-heavy on the water and in flight due to the large bill. They feed, sometimes swinging their heads from side to side in a sweeping action, on crustaceans, insects, plankton and seeds which are sifted through the large bill.

Jan	Feb	Mar	Apr	May	Jun	Jul	Aug	Sep	Oct	Nov	Dec

Garganey

Anas querquedula
38 cm

duck

drake

The Garganey is a small, fast-flying, dabbling duck and is a regular passage migrant in small numbers.

The drake Garganey in spring is one of the most attractive ducks. Its vivid white stripe over the eye and the black-rimmed, golden feathers on the back make it easy to identify. The female and autumn male are brown all over and very similar to the female Eurasian Teal, though the Garganey has a black line through the eye. This can be rather hard to see and a firm identification can be tricky. In flight, large bluish wing patches are conspicuous.

Although classified as dabbling ducks, Garganeys feed with a skimming action rather than by up-ending. When disturbed they rise quickly from the water with a fast, twisting flight.

| Jan | Feb | Mar | Apr | May | Jun | Jul | Aug | Sep | Oct | Nov | Dec |

Eurasian Teal

Anas crecca
36 cm

duck

drake

The Eurasian Teal is a regular passage migrant and winter visitor to grey water lagoons and coastal areas.

The Eurasian Teal is the smallest of the ducks found in Qatar. In autumn the Eurasian Teal is rather uniformly brown and can be separated from other ducks often just by size. In late winter the drake Teal is easy to identify with its strikingly marked reddish-brown head with a dark green patch, and a yellow spot near the tail. The female is brown.

Teal are agile little birds, dashing off the water when alarmed and turning and twisting in flight. They feed mainly on vegetation, and although dabbling ducks they may be seen grazing in the shallows. The males have a whistling call.

| Jan | Feb | Mar | Apr | May | Jun | Jul | Aug | Sep | Oct | Nov | Dec |

Eurasian Wigeon

Anas penelope
48 cm

duck

drakes

The drake Eurasian Wigeon is easy to recognize with its brownish head with a broad creamy stripe over the crown. The female is dark brown. In flight the Eurasian Wigeon shows white underparts and much white on the upper wing. Equally important for identifying the birds in flight is the characteristic, high-pitched whistle coming from a flock flying over. These ducks fly in a tight flock rather than an open V. They often graze on land. Eurasian Wigeons arrive late in Qatar and are not really common till mid winter.

| Jan | Feb | Mar | Apr | May | Jun | Jul | Aug | Sep | Oct | Nov | Dec |

Common Pochard

Aythya ferina
46 cm

duck

drakes

The Common Pochard is a diving duck and a fairly common winter visitor to grey water lagoons and coastal areas.

The drake is unmistakable with a reddish-brown head, dark brown breast and pale grey back and sides. Females are a nondescript mottled brown and grey, but the peaked head and long bill help to identify them.

Common Pochards are omnivorous, diving for plant material, molluscs, water insects and even small fish. The previous species of ducks (p 150-6) are all dabbling ducks. They cannot dive but are often seen 'up-ending' with head under water searching for food and only rump and tail sticking up.

| Jan | Feb | Mar | Apr | May | Jun | Jul | Aug | Sep | Oct | Nov | Dec |

Ferruginous Duck

Aythya nyroca
40 cm

duck

drake

Globally threatened, the Ferruginous Duck is a scarce localized breeder in Qatar, frequenting wetlands such as Abu Nakhla.

The drake Ferruginous Duck is rufous-brown, with a conspicuous white eye, and is sometimes called the White-eyed Duck. The female is more of a chocolate brown with a brown iris. An important identification feature of both male and female is the white rump clearly visible when the birds are seen from the side, and the white wingbar conspicuous in flight. Being a diving duck, the Ferruginous Duck can disappear for a considerable time under water as it feeds on seeds and vegetation and small invertebrates. It also dabbles upended for food, often feeding at night.

| Jan | Feb | Mar | Apr | May | Jun | Jul | Aug | Sep | Oct | Nov | Dec |

Tufted Duck

Aythya fuligula
42 cm

duck

drake

The Tufted Duck is a fairly common winter visitor to grey water pools and coastal lagoons. Like the Common Pochard (p 157), it is a true diving duck and omnivorous, feeding on vegetation, molluscs and aquatic insects. It can dive to a considerable depth in search of its favourite shellfish.

The drake Tufted Duck is an elegant-looking bird. The plumage is shining black with a large white patch on the side and a bright yellow eye. It sports a black tuft on the nape of the neck, hence the species' name. The white sides may be mottled grey in young males. The female is dark brown often with white feathering around the base of the bill, which in both sexes is grey with a black tip. Tufted Ducks can be more trusting of humans than other ducks.

| Jan | Feb | Mar | Apr | May | Jun | Jul | Aug | Sep | Oct | Nov | Dec |

Common Shelduck

Tadorna tadorna
60 cm

Common Shelduck are winter visitors in Qatar, generally found along the coast, although in small numbers. They are large, rather goose-like birds and their vivid colouring makes them instantly recognisable.

The neck, body and back are pure white with a dark green head, black markings on the back, a bright chestnut breast band and pink legs. The slightly upturned bill is red, and drakes have a small, swollen knob on the bill in front of the forehead during the breeding season.

These ducks fly more slowly than other species of ducks, flying low over water. They frequent grey water lagoons such as Abu Nakhla and coastal areas between Doha and Al Ruwais, where flocks of 15-20 birds can occur.

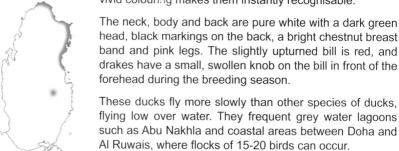

| Jan | Feb | Mar | Apr | May | Jun | Jul | Aug | Sep | Oct | Nov | Dec |

Ruddy Shelduck

Tadorna ferruginea
65 cm

Small flocks numbering up to ten birds have been recorded as annual winter visitors in the area of Simaisma and Al Khor on the east coast. The name refers to their rich orange-red plumage. The head is a pale buff and the wings have black flight feathers and a green speculum. Together with the black legs and beak, the handsome colouring makes Ruddy Shelducks instantly identifiable.

Jan	Feb	Mar	Apr	May	Jun	Jul	Aug	Sep	Oct	Nov	Dec

Greylag Goose

Anser anser
80 cm

An occasional winter visitor, the Greylag Goose is the largest of the geese migrating between Asia and Europe. It frequents inland grey water wetlands such as those at Abu Nakhla and Al Khor. In some winters flocks of about half a dozen birds can be found. A bulky bird, it has a large head, a pink triangular bill and pink legs. (The race found in Qatar breeds in Eastern Europe and further eastward; the western European race has an orange-yellow bill.) The head is grey.

They are noisy birds and their cackling and honking can be heard from a long distance. Greylag Geese can be easy to identify in flight from the pale leading edge to the wings.

Jan	Feb	Mar	Apr	May	Jun	Jul	Aug	Sep	Oct	Nov	Dec

Greater White-fronted Goose

Anser albifrons
70 cm

A large grey goose slightly smaller than the Greylag Goose, the Greater White-fronted Goose is an occasional winter visitor to coasts and grey water wetland areas. The colouring is mainly a mid-brown with lighter brown upper wing coverts. If seen well on the ground the adults can be distinguished from the Greylag Goose by the white patch at the base of the pink bill, dark head and conspicuous dark bars on the belly. The legs are a bright orange. Immature birds are more dull coloured and may only have a hint of white at the base of the bill. In Qatar most records are of single birds or occasionally a family party of 4-5 birds.

Jan	Feb	Mar	Apr	May	Jun	Jul	Aug	Sep	Oct	Nov	Dec

Egyptian Goose

Alopochen aegyptiaca
68 cm

A scarce resident or possibly a feral escape, the Egyptian Goose is a large, brownish-buff bird with a pale neck and face and a prominent chocolate brown eye-patch. Both sexes share the same colouring. Its generic name *Alopochen* refers to the 'foxy' red colour of its wings, which also bear prominent white patches, visible in flight, and a glossy green speculum.

Jan	Feb	Mar	Apr	May	Jun	Jul	Aug	Sep	Oct	Nov	Dec

Purple Swamphen

Porphyrio porphyrio
50 cm

A breeding population of these large, vividly coloured waterbirds, probably descended from escaped birds or else deliberately introduced, is established in the wetlands at Abu Nakhla. Twice the size of a Common Moorhen (p 166), with red legs, the plumage is an iridescent purplish-blue against which the powerful scarlet bill and frontal shield stand out.

Despite its lack of webbed feet the Purple Swamphen is a good swimmer, although it is more often seen paddling in shallow water or walking on the mudbanks. It is a shy bird but its colour makes it easily visible as it clambers among the reeds, searching for young shoots and other vegetable matter. It will also eat small fish and invertebrates.

Jan	Feb	Mar	Apr	May	Jun	Jul	Aug	Sep	Oct	Nov	Dec

Common Moorhen

Gallinula chloropus
32 cm

An abundant breeding resident, the Common Moorhen can be found on almost any open water, from the lakes at the Doha Golf Club to grey water lagoons at Abu Nakhla and Al Khor, where congregations of 150+ have been recorded. Their nests are hidden among the reeds.

Adult males and females are alike and have a black body with a white stripe on the side, bright green legs and a yellow and red bill. Juveniles develop from black fluffy chicks into young birds with brown colouring, and a brown bill. Moorhens have a habit of swimming with body bent forwards which can be used to distinguish them.

These birds spend much time hidden in the reeds, from where croaking and splashing sounds can be heard as the birds fight for territory and chase each other. Quite often though, they can be seen right out in the open swimming with nodding movements and with tail pointing upwards. Their diet includes vegetable matter and invertebrates.

Jan	Feb	Mar	Apr	May	Jun	Jul	Aug	Sep	Oct	Nov	Dec

Eurasian Coot

Fulica atra
36 cm

The Eurasian Coot is a winter visitor and a breeding resident. Adult birds are instantly recognisable with their sooty-black plumage and white frontal shield and bill.

Outside the breeding season, Eurasian Coots are social birds that are often seen in small flocks. The Eurasian Coot spends more time out in the open than the Common Moorhen. It takes off noisily, running across the water surface with beating wings before becoming air-borne. When swimming on a lagoon and up-ending to seek food in the shallow water, it resembles a duck, but Eurasian Coots - like Common Moorhens - belong to the rail family. The diet includes invertebrates and water plants, for which it will sometimes dive.

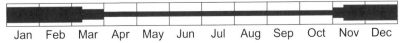

| Jan | Feb | Mar | Apr | May | Jun | Jul | Aug | Sep | Oct | Nov | Dec |

167

Water Rail

Rallus aquaticus
25 cm

An uncommonly seen winter visitor, this shy and secretive bird is more often heard than seen as it skulks in the reeds surrounding grey water lagoons. It

sometimes visits quiet parks and gardens where irrigation spills. It is most likely to be seen at dusk and dawn, and will sometimes sun and preen itself. Smaller and sleeker than Common Moorhens (p 166), Water Rails have dark brown mottled upperparts, the brown extending up the neck to the top of the head, while the sides of the head and underparts are a slate blue. The flanks are barred in black and white.

They feed on invertebrates, vegetation and seeds. When disturbed into flight they fly only a short distance, wings fluttering and long legs dangling and often trailing the surface of the water, before disappearing into cover.

Jan	Feb	Mar	Apr	May	Jun	Jul	Aug	Sep	Oct	Nov	Dec

Spotted Crake

Porzana porzana
21 cm

The Spotted Crake is an uncommonly seen passage migrant, especially in autumn, frequenting the reed beds on grey water lagoons. Like the Water Rail, it is a shy bird and does not often emerge from the reed thickets. To see this bird one must wait patiently in the early morning or late afternoon at the edge of a lagoon where the birds forage in the mixture of mud and dead plant material.

In appearance, the Spotted Crake is not unlike a small bantam chicken; it has a rounded, plump body with a short, upward-pointing tail and a short yellow bill with a reddish base. The plumage is greyish-brown, heavily spotted with white on the cheeks and underparts. Wings and back are a darker brown with markings. The legs are green. Juveniles lack the grey on the head and have white on the throat and pale creamy-brown underparts with less conspicuous whitish spots.

| Jan | Feb | Mar | Apr | May | Jun | Jul | Aug | Sep | Oct | Nov | Dec |

Common Snipe

Gallinago gallinago
26 cm

With their cryptic coloration, Common Snipes can be difficult to spot as they tend to stay in dense cover or blend in with the surroundings. The Common Snipe is a common passage migrant and winter visitor to grey water lagoons throughout Qatar such as the Abu Nakhla ponds and Al Khor wetlands, and well-watered farmlands as at Mukaines.

The Common Snipe is easy to identify. The long straight bill and golden stripes on the crown and back separate it from all other birds except Jack Snipes. If threatened the Common Snipe may first 'freeze' to make itself invisible, trusting to camouflage, and then explode into zig-zagging flight with loud harsh calls. A white trailing edge to the wings can be seen in flight.

| Jan | Feb | Mar | Apr | May | Jun | Jul | Aug | Sep | Oct | Nov | Dec |

Jack Snipe

Lymnocryptes minimus
18 cm

The Jack Snipe is an occasional passage migrant to grey water lagoons. It is much less common than the Common Snipe, and can be hard to find due to its secretive habits.

Superficially, the Jack Snipe looks like the Common Snipe, but is much smaller, and relatively shorter billed and shorter tailed, giving it a dumpy appearance. If seen at close range the central crown stripe is dark brown whereas that of the Common Snipe is yellowish brown. When humans approach, a Jack Snipe crouches and freezes, relying on its excellent camouflage, and will not take off till one almost steps on the bird. Unlike the zig-zagging flight of the Common Snipe, that of the Jack Snipe is usually short and curves back down to land not far away. Most records in Qatar are of single birds that were accidentally disturbed near damp ground.

| Jan | Feb | Mar | Apr | May | Jun | Jul | Aug | Sep | Oct | Nov | Dec |

171

Black-winged Stilt

Himantopus himantopus
40 cm

The Black-winged Stilt is a common, but localized breeding resident and a more widespread passage migrant and winter visitor. The birds frequent grey water lagoons, preferably those with some cover. They can usually be seen at the Al Khor wetland and Abu Nakhla pools, often in flocks of up to 100 or more, feeding on insects which they pick delicately from the water surface or just below it. If disturbed they fly off, calling noisily. They are wary birds and keep their distance from humans.

The Black-winged Stilt is unmistakable with its extraordinarily long, fragile-looking red legs, thin straight bill and black and white plumage. In flight the legs extend well beyond the tail. It is an opportunistic breeder, and small numbers may breed when they find the habitat to their liking, such as newly formed water spillage areas.

Jan	Feb	Mar	Apr	May	Jun	Jul	Aug	Sep	Oct	Nov	Dec

172

Pied Avocet

Recurvirostra avocetta
42 cm

The Pied Avocet is a passage migrant and winter visitor, seen at sites on the east coast. A few pairs have recently been recorded as breeding here at grey water lagoons.

This large wading bird is easy to identify with its black and white plumage and long, delicate, up-curved bill. It usually feeds by scything the bill from side to side on the surface of the water, a distinctive method of feeding unique to avocets. The diet consists of crustaceans and insects. If disturbed, the flock takes off, circles around a few times and settles down again further away. Like the Black-winged Stilt it is noisy and when taking off it calls a repeated '*bluit bluit*,' not as scolding as the call of the stilt.

| Jan | Feb | Mar | Apr | May | Jun | Jul | Aug | Sep | Oct | Nov | Dec |

Ruff

Philomachus pugnax
22-28 cm

The Ruff is a common passage migrant and winter visitor. It frequents grey water lagoons, and is also found on farmlands. It is usually encountered in small flocks.

The Ruff derives its name from the collar of ruffed up feathers displayed by male birds in breeding plumage when they gather at 'leks' to dance and joust. While in Qatar these ruffs are not present, however, and the Ruff is a rather nondescript bird. Good field marks are the smallish head with short, slightly down-curved bill. There is usually a white mark on the face at the base of the bill and the underparts can be chequered brown, grey and off-white. The legs are long and orange in colour. In flight, a horseshoe-shaped white patch is visible on the rump. Males are considerably bigger than females. The Ruff is mostly silent but may occasionally give a low, two-note whistle.

| Jan | Feb | Mar | Apr | May | Jun | Jul | Aug | Sep | Oct | Nov | Dec |

Common Sandpiper

Actitis hypoleucos
20 cm

The Common Sandpiper is a common passage migrant and winter visitor to rocky shores, grey water lagoons and pools at the Doha Golf Course. It prefers areas with some sheltering rocks or vegetation rather than open tidal mud-flats, and is also seen in coastal areas with mangrove forests and even on lawns in large hotel gardens.

A long-tailed, short-legged wader, the Common Sandpiper has a typical 'crouched' stance and constantly bobs its rear-end up and down. In appearance it is a dark greyish-buff above with clean white breast and underparts. The flight action is characteristic: a few rapid wing beats followed by a glide with wings held downward. The call is a high-pitched whistle. The closest confusion species is the Green Sandpiper (p 180).

Jan	Feb	Mar	Apr	May	Jun	Jul	Aug	Sep	Oct	Nov	Dec

Spotted Redshank

Tringa erythropus
30 cm

late spring

winter

The Spotted Redshank is a regular passage migrant and winter visitor. It is found at inland grey water lagoons and at saltwater habitats.

In breeding plumage in late spring the Spotted Redshank is unmistakable - black all over, with small white spots freckling the back and wings, a white

wedge on the back which is visible when the bird is in flight, and black legs tinged with red. In winter it changes to very pale grey upperparts and white underparts, against which its red legs are conspicuous. A darker eye-stripe is visible when the bird is seen in a good light.

The bill of the Spotted Redshank is long and thin and is mostly black, with only the inner half of the lower mandible being red, and a slight downward curvature at the tip. In flight it does not have a white trailing edge to the wings as does its slightly smaller relative the Common Redshank. The flight call is a distinctive whistling '*tjo-wheeet.*'

| Jan | Feb | Mar | Apr | May | Jun | Jul | Aug | Sep | Oct | Nov | Dec |

Common Redshank

Tringa totanus
28 cm

late spring

winter

The Common Redshank is an abundant passage migrant and winter visitor and is one of the most common waders in Qatar. It is found at grey water lagoons up and down the country, beaches, mangrove forests and tidal mudflats.

A medium sized grey-brown wader, the Common Redshank has long orange-red legs - hence its name - and a straight red bill. The plumage has prominent dark spots. The legs retain their orange-red colour all year round unlike those of the Spotted Redshank.

It is at home anywhere there is water, fresh or salt, and is active looking for food in shallow water or on the mudflats. It sometimes bobs its tail like the Common Sandpiper. If disturbed it flies off, piping loudly '*deu deu.*' In flight a white trailing edge to the wings is conspicuous. Any trip to a suitable habitat between August and May should give sightings of this bird.

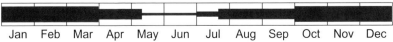

| Jan | Feb | Mar | Apr | May | Jun | Jul | Aug | Sep | Oct | Nov | Dec |

177

Marsh Sandpiper

Tringa stagnatilis
24 cm

The Marsh Sandpiper is a fairly common passage migrant and winter visitor. The main habitat is grey water lagoons and exposed mudflats near mangroves, but one shouldn't expect to see it on open sandy beaches.

Superficially the Marsh Sandpiper looks like a Common Greenshank, but it is a smaller and more delicate bird with less white on the back and long, yellowish legs. In winter the plumage is uniformly greyish-brown above with a lighter underside. The bill is straight and very thin and used for probing for the invertebrates which provide the bird's main diet. In flight its long legs project beyond the tail. The bird does not have the Common Greenshank's loud, scolding call. Marsh Sandpipers are normally encountered singly or in small numbers; a flock of more than half-a-dozen birds would be unusual.

| Jan | Feb | Mar | Apr | May | Jun | Jul | Aug | Sep | Oct | Nov | Dec |

Common Greenshank

Tringa nebularia

32 cm

The Common Greenshank is a common passage migrant and winter visitor, with occasional non-breeding birds staying over summer. It frequents inland grey water lagoons as well as beaches, mangrove forests and tidal mudflats, where it hunts for small fish and invertebrates.

A stockily-built and active wader, the Common Greenshank has a heavy, slightly up-turned bill and greenish legs. The bill is long and dark with a grey base. The upperparts are dark grey with a lighter underside and white rump, and in flight it shows a white wedge up the back.

It is rather shy and when disturbed takes off and calls noisily with a three-syllable: '*tjiu tjiu tjiu*.' Common Greenshanks and Common Redshanks (p 177) are found in similar habitats, but the Common Greenshank is not as numerous. It is mostly seen singly or in small groups.

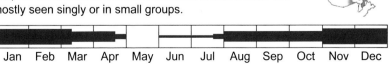

| Jan | Feb | Mar | Apr | May | Jun | Jul | Aug | Sep | Oct | Nov | Dec |

Green Sandpiper

Tringa ochropus
23 cm

The Green Sandpiper is a common passage migrant and winter visitor, though less numerous than the previous species. It is a shy bird and often not seen until it takes to flight. The preferred habitats are similar to those of the Wood Sandpiper: grey water lagoons and pools such as those at Abu Nakhla and Al Khor.

Green Sandpipers most closely resemble Common Sandpipers (p 175) in size and 'jizz'. However they are darker above contrasting with the white rump seen in flight, and lack the white wing bar. When young Green Sandpipers arrive in early autumn they look almost black on the upperparts and compared to Wood Sandpipers they lack the white spots on the back. In flight the Green Sandpiper shows distinctive black underwings and a conspicuous white rump. The flight call is a characteristic, metallic 'do-eet weet weet.' Green Sandpipers are usually seen in ones and twos around the edge of pools.

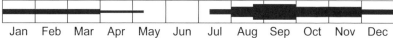

| Jan | Feb | Mar | Apr | May | Jun | Jul | Aug | Sep | Oct | Nov | Dec |

Wood Sandpiper

Tringa glareola
20 cm

The Wood Sandpiper is an abundant passage migrant and winter visitor to inland freshwater habitats throughout the country, including grey water lagoons and farmlands. It is rarely found along the beaches or on tidal mudflats.

The long-necked, long-legged Wood Sandpiper is similar to the previously described sandpipers, but it has a shorter bill and is more spotted on the upperparts. The distinctive light eye-stripe, extending towards the back of the neck, aids identification, as do the yellowish legs and thin sharply-pointed bill. Summer and winter plumages look similar, though it is slightly duller in winter, and overall it is lighter than the Green Sandpiper.

In flight the Wood Sandpiper has a white rump. It can call noisily when feeding rights are being challenged by other birds, or if a bird-watcher approaches too closely. The call is a high whistle of three notes: *'jiff-jiff-jiff.'*

Jan	Feb	Mar	Apr	May	Jun	Jul	Aug	Sep	Oct	Nov	Dec

Whimbrel

Numenius phaeopus
40 cm

The Whimbrel is an abundant passage migrant and winter visitor to coastal areas throughout Qatar. The Whimbrel is also often found in town parks and road verges in winter, probing the damp lawns for invertebrates. It is more often seen than the Eurasian Curlew which is more commonly found along the coast.

Resembling a smaller version of a Eurasian Curlew, the Whimbrel has a shorter, more down-curved bill than the Curlew. It is a slightly darker bird than the Curlew, with pale underparts, and distinctive brown streaks on the crown. If these crown streaks are clearly seen then the identification has been clinched! In flight a white V-shaped patch is visible on its back above the tail.

The flight call is entirely different from that of the Eurasian Curlew, a series of excited-sounding repeated '*bi-bi-bi-bi-bi*' instead of the distinctive, haunting call of the Curlew. Whimbrels usually fly with faster wingbeats than do Curlews.

| Jan | Feb | Mar | Apr | May | Jun | Jul | Aug | Sep | Oct | Nov | Dec |

Eurasian Curlew

Numenius arquata
55 cm

The Eurasian Curlew is a common passage migrant and winter visitor. The bird is easy to find on tidal mudflats on the east coast, as well as on beaches and sometimes on farmlands.

The Eurasian Curlew is a large, brownish-mottled, greyish-toned wader with a very long, down-curved bill. The nearest confusion species is the Whimbrel, but the Eurasian Curlew lacks that species' striped crown and has a much longer bill. In flight, both species have a white rump and a white wedge extending up the back. The flight tends to be slower than that of Whimbrels. The piping call of the Eurasian Curlew is a haunting '*curl-eueeee*', lower pitched than the Whimbrel's urgent-sounding call notes '*bi-bi-bi-bi-bi*'.

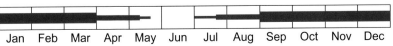

| Jan | Feb | Mar | Apr | May | Jun | Jul | Aug | Sep | Oct | Nov | Dec |

Black-tailed Godwit

Limosa limosa
42 cm

The Black-tailed Godwit is an uncommon passage migrant to Qatar. It is a large wader with a very long, straight bill, slightly up-curved at the tip, and long, dark-

ish legs. On the ground it resembles its close relative the Bar-tailed Godwit, but is slightly bigger. It takes an experienced birder to distinguish between the two, but the Black-tailed has a longer and more solid-looking bill than the Bar-tailed Godwit. While in Qatar the Black-tailed Godwit is uniformly grey on the upperparts.

In flight, the Black-tailed Godwit shows a prominent white wing bar and a white tail with a broad, black band at the tip. It is never numerous and flocks rarely exceed ten birds. The call when disturbed is a loud, repeated '*wicka-wicka-wicka*'.

| Jan | Feb | Mar | Apr | May | Jun | Jul | Aug | Sep | Oct | Nov | Dec |

Bar-tailed Godwit

Limosa lapponica
38 cm

winter plumage

summer plumage

The Bar-tailed Godwit is a common passage migrant and winter visitor regularly seen along the coasts of Qatar. It can be found on beaches and tidal mudflats.

This large wader can be identified by its long legs and very long, slightly up-turned bill. In autumn and winter it is uniformly grey, but by March begins to change into its brick-red breeding plumage. The tail has fine horizontal barring, seen best when the bird is in flight. Bar-tailed Godwits are usually seen in flocks on the beach or on the mudflats, where the birds probe deeply with their long bills in search of food. In both species of godwits, their long legs and long bill give them an edge over other waders in probing that bit deeper into the mud.

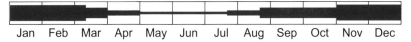

| Jan | Feb | Mar | Apr | May | Jun | Jul | Aug | Sep | Oct | Nov | Dec |

185

Crab-plover

Dromas ardeola
38 cm

The Crab-plover, mainly a passage migrant in Qatar, is a 'special' bird for many birders in the Arabian Gulf. It is a 'relict' species, i.e. the last survivor of a group of birds now extinct through evolution, and the only member of the genus *Dromas*.

With its striking black and white plumage, heavy black pointed bill and long pale blue legs, the Crab-plover is unmistakable. Flocks of Crab-plovers, usu-

ally containing adult birds and juveniles begging for food, can sometimes be seen on intertidal flats and sand spits near Simaisma on the east coast. The young birds have the same plumage pattern as adults but with more grey on the crown and the wings. Crab-plovers feed at night as well as during the day.

Crab-plovers feed like other plovers, with a short run or strutting walk followed by a pause. The bill is unique among waders: the birds' diet consists entirely of molluscs and crabs, which they stab with their great bills and then break up by pounding them.

| Jan | Feb | Mar | Apr | May | Jun | Jul | Aug | Sep | Oct | Nov | Dec |

Eurasian Oystercatcher

Haematopus ostralegus
42 cm

The Eurasian Oystercatcher is a passage migrant and winter visitor to open sandy beaches and tidal mudflats.

This handsome, large, black and white bird with bright orange/red bill and legs is one of the most easily recognizable birds at the beach. The plumage does not vary much from winter to summer except for a horizontal white line on the throat that disappears in summer. Immature birds are duller in colour and the band on the throat is incomplete.

Eurasian Oystercatchers are often found in small flocks feeding just at the water's edge. If disturbed they fly off calling loudly - '*kibeek-kibeek*' - to land further down the beach and resume feeding. The strong bill is used for prising open or breaking molluscs.

Jan	Feb	Mar	Apr	May	Jun	Jul	Aug	Sep	Oct	Nov	Dec

Grey Plover

Pluvialis squatarola
29 cm

breeding
plumage

winter
plumage

The Grey Plover is an abundant passage migrant and winter visitor along the beaches and tidal mudflats. The bird is aptly named at least as far as its winter plumage is concerned, being uniformly greyish-brown on back and wings, with a paler front. The bill is rather short for a wader. Good identification marks are the black axillaries (underside of the wings where they join the body) seen when the bird is in flight. In late spring, just before the birds start heading north, the Grey Plover changes into its handsome breeding plumage with sooty-black face, breast and underparts, and white framing the black face with a sprinkling of grey on top of the head.

Grey Plovers are less gregarious than other plovers, feeding widely dispersed along a shore, rather than in flocks, as they hunt for molluscs, crustaceans and insects.

| Jan | Feb | Mar | Apr | May | Jun | Jul | Aug | Sep | Oct | Nov | Dec |

Kentish Plover

Charadrius alexandrinus
16 cm

winter
plumage

female
at nest

male, breeding
plumage

The Kentish Plover is a breeding resident on sandy beaches on the mainland, around the fringes of the grey water lagoons and on offshore islands. It is also an abundant passage migrant and winter visitor throughout coastal areas and grey water lagoons. The nests are scrapes in sand or gravel and the eggs so well camouflaged that great care has to be taken to avoid treading on them. When feeding, the birds run very fast, seeming to scoot along the shore, pausing to peck in the sand before running on again.

Unlike the Common Ringed Plover (p 192) and Little Ringed Plover (p 110) the Kentish Plover has an incomplete black breast band. In breeding plumage there are two sharply demarcated black lines on either side of the breast, a black horizontal line on the forehead and a neat tan-coloured cap on the head. Outside the spring breeding season, these bands may become more diffuse. The white hind neck distinguishes the Kentish Plover from the two sand plovers (pp 190-1) in winter. Unlike the Common Ringed and Little Ringed Plovers, Kentish Plovers have very dark legs. It is the smallest of the plovers in Qatar.

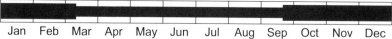

| Jan | Feb | Mar | Apr | May | Jun | Jul | Aug | Sep | Oct | Nov | Dec |

Lesser Sand Plover

Charadrius mongolus
20 cm

breeding
plumage

winter
plumage

The Lesser Sand Plover is an abundant passage migrant and winter visitor, feeding along the sandy beaches and tidal mudflats. It is one of the most common birds of the coast.

This species is medium in size between the Kentish Plover (p 189) and the Greater Sand Plover, but size is a difficult field mark unless the different species are seen next to each other. The Lesser Sand Plover has a finer bill and shorter legs than the Greater. They feed on insects, crustaceans and worms, running and pausing rather than probing the sand as sandpipers do.

Birds seen in late spring and early autumn have black foreheads and rufous markings on the neck and breast, while winter birds lack rufous markings and have dark breast bands. Lesser Sand Plovers normally outnumber their larger relatives.

| Jan | Feb | Mar | Apr | May | Jun | Jul | Aug | Sep | Oct | Nov | Dec |

Greater Sand Plover

Charadrius leschenaultii
24 cm

breeding plumage

winter plumage

Like the previous species, the Greater Sand Plover is a common passage migrant and winter visitor to beaches and tidal mudflats throughout Qatar, with a few birds staying all year. In most years it is rather less numerous than the Lesser Sand Plover.

Great skill and care is needed to distinguish between the Greater and Lesser Sand Plovers, and only with experience of both species can identifications be safe. The Greater is a stockier and larger bird with a longer, heavier bill and longer legs but this is really only noticeable when the two species occur side by side. In late spring both species develop rufous markings on the head and breast as they move into summer plumage, but the Greater Sand Plover can be distinguished by its white forehead.

| Jan | Feb | Mar | Apr | May | Jun | Jul | Aug | Sep | Oct | Nov | Dec |

Common Ringed Plover

Charadrius hiaticula
19 cm

The Common Ringed Plover is an abundant passage migrant and winter visitor, with a few non-breeding birds staying over summer. This species is more coastal than its smaller relative, the Little Ringed Plover (p 110), and is found on beaches and tidal mudflats, but it also occurs on the flooded sabkha wetlands at Al Khor.

This bird is normally seen in small flocks on a sandy beach. The lack of an eye-ring and orange legs distinguish it from the Little Ringed Plover. The short bill is red with a black tip. In flight, a conspicuous white wing bar can be seen. The Common Ringed Plover usually has a complete black breast band. Plovers feed by a run-and-pause action, whereas sandpipers use a 'sewing-machine' technique: dipping their bills repeatedly into the sand. The call of the Common Ringed Plover is a soft 2-syllable whistle, '*too-weep*', whereas the Little Ringed Plover's call is a loud monosyllabic '*kew.*'

| Jan | Feb | Mar | Apr | May | Jun | Jul | Aug | Sep | Oct | Nov | Dec |

192

Terek Sandpiper

Xenus cinereus
23 cm

The Terek Sandpiper is a common passage migrant and winter visitor, with many sightings of non-breeding birds staying over summer. Look for this wader on beaches, tidal mudflats and mangrove forests on the east and west coasts.

This species can be identified both from its appearance and its habits. It is rather dumpy, and short-legged for its size, and has a long, slightly up-turned bill with an orange base darkening to black along the length. The back, face and breast are grey in all plumages, and the belly is white. The legs are yellowish-orange. The stance is rather horizontal. The call is a clear, fluting whistle.

Terek Sandpipers are very active running over the mud-flats, stopping suddenly to look for food. In flight, a white trailing edge to the wings can be seen. In most cases, the birds are seen singly, but sizeable flocks can be seen at high tide roosts.

| Jan | Feb | Mar | Apr | May | Jun | Jul | Aug | Sep | Oct | Nov | Dec |

Little Stint

Calidris minuta
13 cm

early autumn

winter

A tiny wader, the Little Stint is an abundant passage migrant and winter visitor to inland grey water lagoons as well as beaches and tidal mudflats. It is found along all Qatar's coastline. This is the most abundant small wader in Qatar. It often occurs in flocks of 30 or more.

The Little Stint can be tricky to separate from other small sandpipers, but its small size, black legs and rapid movements distinguish it from all other waders except the Temminck's Stint. Like that species, the Little Stint has a short, straight bill, but they can be told apart by the more mottled back pattern and black legs of the Little Stint. On grey water lagoons the two species are often found side by side. In late spring, the Little Stint develops its summer plumage with colour on face, neck, breast and wings varying from a soft orange to a warm brown and numerous dark reddish spots on the upperside. The call is a shrill, rapid '*stit-stit-stit*' with an occasional short trill.

| Jan | Feb | Mar | Apr | May | Jun | Jul | Aug | Sep | Oct | Nov | Dec |

Temminck's Stint

Calidris temminckii
13 cm

The Temminck's Stint is a much less common passage migrant and winter visitor than the Little Stint to grey water lagoons, pools and flooded areas. It is not so often found on coastal, saltwater lagoons or on tidal mudflats.

The Temminck's Stint looks like a greyish Little Stint, and the two species are often found together at grey water pools. Seen side by side, the Temminck's Stint has shorter yellowish green legs and slightly longer wings than the Little Stint. The outer tail feathers are white whereas the Little Stint's outer tail feathers are grey and it has black legs. The Temminck's Stint has a more uniformly coloured back, unlike the Little Stint's more scalloped appearance. When taking off, Temminck's Stints utter a high-pitched prolonged trill compared to the Little Stints' single-noted call and short trill.

Jan	Feb	Mar	Apr	May	Jun	Jul	Aug	Sep	Oct	Nov	Dec

195

Dunlin

Calidris alpina
18 cm

summer

winter

autumn

One of the most common and numerous waders in Qatar, Dunlins are found along all beaches and tidal mudflats during passage migration and in winter. They are highly gregarious birds, often forming large flocks and feeding with a 'sewing machine' action, picking molluscs, worms and small crustaceans from the sand.

During the winter months the Dunlin is in dull, greyish plumage and is not so easy to identify. Good field marks include a longer bill that curves downward very slightly at the tip and greyish sides to the neck. In early autumn and late spring adults in breeding plumage have a black patch on the belly and brownish-red back with darker spots. No other wader of similar size has this black patch. In flight, the Dunlin shows a black vertical line on the rump.

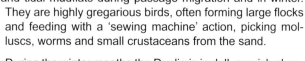

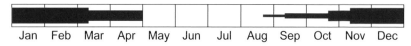

Jan	Feb	Mar	Apr	May	Jun	Jul	Aug	Sep	Oct	Nov	Dec

Curlew Sandpiper

Calidris ferruginea
19 cm

winter

summer

autumn

The Curlew Sandpiper is a common passage migrant. Autumn birds start to arrive in Qatar in late July. They can be found along the beaches and on tidal mudflats.

Late spring and early autumn birds will be in their breeding plumage, and head, neck, breast and belly are a rich chestnut with brownish-red wings. In non-breeding plumage the Curlew Sandpiper closely resembles a Dunlin. Field marks to look out for include a long, down-curved bill, slightly larger and more slender body and, in flight, a white rump. Compared to the Dunlin, the bill is longer and curves in its entire length whereas the bill of the Dunlin curves only near the tip, and the Curlew Sandpiper can feed in slightly deeper water.

| Jan | Feb | Mar | Apr | May | Jun | Jul | Aug | Sep | Oct | Nov | Dec |

Sanderling

Calidris alba
17 cm

summer

winter

The Sanderling is a frequent passage migrant and winter visitor to sandy shore-lines and tidal mudflats in Qatar. Look for this small, plump, energetic wader in

small flocks just at the water's edge. The birds run restlessly along the waterline, dodging the incoming waves and snatching small animals thrown up by the sea as the waves retreat.

This species is the palest and one of the smallest of the sandpipers in Qatar. In a mixed flock they can look almost white with a small black patch on the front of the wing. The short bill and the legs are black. The summer plumage, which may be seen during late spring and August passage, features a distinctive reddish colouring to the head and breast and darker scalloped markings on the breast. The flight call is a distinctive '*plick*'.

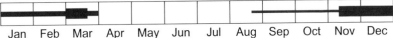

| Jan | Feb | Mar | Apr | May | Jun | Jul | Aug | Sep | Oct | Nov | Dec |

Broad-billed Sandpiper

Limicola falcinellus
17 cm

early autumn

The Broad-billed Sandpiper is a regular passage migrant, but not as common or as numerous as the other small sandpipers. Good places to look for this bird include shorelines and tidal mudflats on the east coast. It does not often mix with other sandpipers, usually occurring singly or in small flocks.

Slightly smaller than a Dunlin (p 196), it is rather short-legged with a black bill that curves down slightly at the tip. Seen straight from the front the bill does indeed look broad, as the bird's name suggests. An excellent field mark is a double supercilium over each eye. In fresh autumn plumage in September, the bird looks very dark on the upper-parts with a white belly. Later in the autumn, it is more uniformly grey above.

Jan	Feb	Mar	Apr	May	Jun	Jul	Aug	Sep	Oct	Nov	Dec

Ruddy Turnstone

Arenaria interpres
23 cm

summer

winter

The Ruddy Turnstone, a small wader, is a frequent passage migrant and winter visitor along the coasts and on tidal mudflats in Qatar.

The stockily-built and short-legged Ruddy Turnstone derives its name from its habit of using its short conical bill to turn over small stones to look for food, mainly invertebrates, underneath. It is easy to identify from the striking black and white pattern on its head and breast. The legs are bright orange. Females are rather more subdued in colouring. In winter the upperparts of the plumage are dark greyish-brown with paler edges and diffuse facial markings. In spring the summer plumage may be seen; this includes striking chestnut-coloured markings on the back. Ruddy Turnstones are often found in small groups of 3-6 individuals.

Jan	Feb	Mar	Apr	May	Jun	Jul	Aug	Sep	Oct	Nov	Dec

Red-necked Phalarope

Phalaropus lobatus
18 cm

summer

autumn

The Red-necked Phalarope is a regular passage migrant in Qatar in small numbers. It is a bird of the open sea and on shore pools – it has the curious and distinctive habit of spinning around in shallow water to swirl up plankton and tiny crustaceans from the bottom, which it pecks up at lightning speed with its needle-thin, sharply pointed bill. Occasionally, Red-necked Phalaropes turn up at freshwater pools. Unlike other waders, Red-necked Phalaropes have lobed toes which enable them to swim strongly.

Red-necked Phalaropes have a red neck only when in breeding plumage. Females are larger and more colourful than males, however during most of their time in Qatar the birds are greyish with a broad black line through the eye. They are rather tame and can often be approached quite closely.

Jan	Feb	Mar	Apr	May	Jun	Jul	Aug	Sep	Oct	Nov	Dec

Caspian Gull
Steppe Gull

Larus cachinnans
Larus barabensis
62 cm

Steppe Gulls

Caspian Gulls

These two gull along with Heuglin's Gull are often just referred to as 'large white-headed gulls' as they are very similar. Immature birds are almost impossible to tell apart. All three species are believed to be regular winter visitors to coastal areas of Qatar.

Adult Caspian and Steppe Gulls are slightly smaller and have a smaller bill and smaller eyes than Heuglin's Gulls along with a more rounded head, giving them a 'gentle' expression. The Caspian Gull is the palest of the three and Heuglin's Gull the darkest. The legs can vary from pale pink to bright yellow. In flight the adult Caspian Gull has less black and more white in the wing tips than the Steppe Gull.

The Caspian Gull's typical appearance when standing is tall and erect, with wing-tips sometimes dropped below horizontal. On the water the narrow wing-tips are often held well clear of the surface.

| Jan | Feb | Mar | Apr | May | Jun | Jul | Aug | Sep | Oct | Nov | Dec |

Heuglin's Gull
Other name: Siberian Gull

Larus heuglini
65 cm

Heuglin's Gull, a third species of the 'large white-headed gull' complex, is a common passage migrant and winter visitor to all coastal areas in Qatar. During the winter months all three species occur, and the largest flocks encountered in recent years have been at the Abu Nakhla pools winter gull roost.

It is very similar in size and appearance to the Caspian and Steppe Gulls, all three are large and have grey wings and mantle, the Heuglin's being the darkest of the three. There is great variation in leg colour, ranging from pale pink to yellow, adding to the confusion. Field marks for the adult Heuglin's Gull include a larger, paler bill and large eyes which give the bird a 'mean' expression. In winter Heuglin's Gulls have extensive dark streaking on the hind neck.

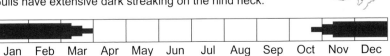

| Jan | Feb | Mar | Apr | May | Jun | Jul | Aug | Sep | Oct | Nov | Dec |

Slender-billed Gull

Chroicocephalus genei
43 cm

The Slender-billed Gull is an abundant winter visitor to sandy beaches and mudflats throughout Qatar. It is most commonly seen on the east coast of the Qatar peninsula and can be seen from the Doha Corniche.

This is a medium-sized gull with a wing-pattern closely resembling that of the Common Black-headed Gull, but is slightly larger and lacks the dark hood of the latter in spring. The dark ear mark is less obvious than on a Common Black-headed Gull in winter, and the bill is longer and the head less rounded. In spring Slender-billed Gulls develop a noticeable pink tinge on the breast. The leg and bill colour varies from black to red.

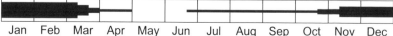

| Jan | Feb | Mar | Apr | May | Jun | Jul | Aug | Sep | Oct | Nov | Dec |

Common Black-headed Gull *Chroicocephalus ridibundus*

38 cm

The Common Black-headed Gull is a common winter visitor, with large flocks sometimes encountered in January and February along the coast at harbours and at inland lagoons. The numbers fluctuate from year to year. It is frequently seen in Doha Bay.

While in Qatar the Common Black-headed Gull does not have the dark brown hood seen in summer. The head is white, sometimes with faint streaks remaining from its summer plumage, and a prominent small dark patch on the ear coverts. A few birds staying till late March and April may begin developing the darker head which gives the bird its name. In winter plumage the bird can look very similar to a Slender-billed Gull, but note the shorter bill and steeper forehead of the Common Black-headed Gull. Both species may have bright red legs and reddish bills.

These gulls are highly gregarious, noisy and quarrelsome, and are almost always seen in flocks. They are opportunist feeders: the varied diet includes fish, worms and other small animals, carrion and waste food left by humans.

| Jan | Feb | Mar | Apr | May | Jun | Jul | Aug | Sep | Oct | Nov | Dec |

Sooty Gull

Larus hemprichii
45 cm

immature

adults

The Sooty Gull is an occasional winter visitor, usually after strong on-shore winds. It breeds in large numbers on off-shore islands off the coast of Oman.

No other gull seen in Qatar has an overall sooty-brown plumage. Immature birds are paler and more mottled brown on the back than adults. Most sightings involve single birds in harbours such as Al Wakra or Al Shamal. In Qatar Sooty Gulls are offshore and coastal birds, feeding on fish or offal discarded by fishermen. It is very unlikely to be found inland.

| Jan | Feb | Mar | Apr | May | Jun | Jul | Aug | Sep | Oct | Nov | Dec |

Great Black-headed Gull

Larus ichtyaetus
68 cm

December

February

A winter visitor to sandy beaches, particularly on the east coast of the Qatar peninsula. It is a late arrival, being found from mid-December to early March.

The Great Black-headed Gull is the biggest gull found in Qatar. When standing next to other gull species on the beach it can appear quite massive. In winter the head is white with blackish streaks, and around February the birds begin to change into their breeding plumage with striking black head which contrasts sharply with the pure white breast and fresh light grey of the back. There are usually small white areas above and below the eyes and it has a colourful yellow bill with a black band. Adult birds also show striking white and black tips to the wings which stand out from the fresh light grey of the back and rest of wings. Immature birds, although mostly grey, also have black wing-tips and a noticeable wide black band on the tail.

Jan	Feb	Mar	Apr	May	Jun	Jul	Aug	Sep	Oct	Nov	Dec

Gull-billed Tern

Gelochelidon nilotica
38 cm

The Gull-billed Tern is a passage migrant and winter visitor. Unlike other terns, it has a rather short, thick bill, black in colour. During autumn and winter the head

is mostly white with a black bar through the eye. In spring and summer the crown is black. These terns are white with wide, pale grey wings, and are stockily built. The legs are black.

Gull-billed Terns are often seen patrolling over the coastal areas and mudflats, swooping down low over the ground and rising again, a behaviour not seen in other terns. They will take small rodents as well as reptiles, insects and crustaceans. They are not as common as other species of terns in Qatar. Gull-billed Terns do not normally plunge-dive for fish like other terns.

| Jan | Feb | Mar | Apr | May | Jun | Jul | Aug | Sep | Oct | Nov | Dec |

Caspian Tern

Hydroprogne caspia
52 cm

winter

summer

The Caspian Tern is an uncommon resident breeder, but a common winter visitor. It is the largest of the terns and is bigger than some of the smaller gulls. The bill is massive and bright coral red with a black tip, making these birds stand out even in a large mixed flock of gulls and terns. The wings are long and pointed and the flight slower than that of other terns, with relaxed wing-beats. In spring and summer the head is black with much of the black retained during winter, but with numerous white streaks, especially on the forehead. The call is deep and raucous. In winter Caspian Terns can be found roosting in groups of up to 20 on east coast beaches. In summer they disperse and are more often found in ones and twos around the Qatar coastline.

| Jan | Feb | Mar | Apr | May | Jun | Jul | Aug | Sep | Oct | Nov | Dec |

Common Tern

Sterna hirundo
35 cm

autumn

spring

The Common Tern is an uncommon passage migrant in spring and autumn. Birds mixed with White-cheeked Terns and other species of terns may be encountered along the coast and at inland water bodies. These elegant, silver-grey and white birds are sometimes referred to as 'sea swallows' because of their long, forked tails. They feed by plunge-diving for fish, usually without hovering first as do some other species of terns.

Adult birds in spring are easy to identify from their red bill with a black tip, black cap and red legs, which remain red throughout the winter, unlike the legs of some other species which change colour. The tail does not extend beyond the wing tips on standing birds. Immature birds are very difficult to separate from immature White-cheeked Terns. A good field mark to look out for is the white rump of the Common Tern, whereas the White-cheeked Tern has a grey rump.

| Jan | Feb | Mar | Apr | May | Jun | Jul | Aug | Sep | Oct | Nov | Dec |

White-cheeked Tern

Sterna repressa
34 cm

autumn

summer

The White-cheeked Tern is a migrant summer breeder on offshore islands, feeding on fish as well as small invertebrates. It plunge-dives for food but will also land on the water and pick fish from just below the surface, or walk around in shallow water. White-cheeked Terns are often seen along the beach in mixed flocks with other terns.

The darkest of the terns in the genus *Sterna*. In breeding plumage this bird is easy to identify from its black cap, white cheeks, dark grey wings and dusky underparts. The bill colour can vary from almost all red to almost all black, and the legs are a dark brownish-red. Immature birds and birds in non-breeding plumage are much paler and are difficult to separate from Common Terns. The White-cheeked Tern, however, has a grey rump in all plumages, where the Common Tern has a white rump.

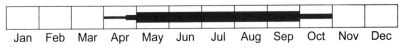

| Jan | Feb | Mar | Apr | May | Jun | Jul | Aug | Sep | Oct | Nov | Dec |

211

Swift Tern
Other name: Greater Crested Tern

Sterna bergii
45 cm

autumn

spring

The Swift Tern is a common passage migrant and winter visitor seen on coastal regions around Qatar. It is a large tern with a long, pointed, straw-coloured bill. In a mixed flock of terns on the beach the Swift Terns normally stand out by their larger size, which also helps to distinguish them from their smaller relatives the Lesser Crested Terns. In spring and summer the head is glossy black with a crest extending onto the hind neck. In winter the forehead turns whitish, but the bill colour is unchanged throughout the year. This species may be seen on both sandy beaches and rocky coastlines and plunge-diving for fish off-shore.

| Jan | Feb | Mar | Apr | May | Jun | Jul | Aug | Sep | Oct | Nov | Dec |

Lesser Crested Tern

Sterna bengalensis
40 cm

The Lesser Crested Tern is an abundant passage migrant and winter visitor in large numbers, with some non-breeding birds staying over summer. Like the Swift Tern and Sandwich Tern (p 214) it feeds by plunge-diving for fish.

This species is quite similar to its close relative the Swift Tern, but the Lesser Crested Tern is much smaller and has a yellow-orange bill. Like its larger relative, it, too, has a black head with a crest in spring and summer, but a white forehead in winter. The grey rump is conspicuous in flight. Normally it is not difficult to identify in mixed flocks of terns, but you have to scan through all birds carefully. Quite a few will then be found to have yellow-orange bills.

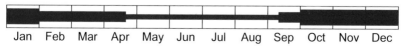

| Jan | Feb | Mar | Apr | May | Jun | Jul | Aug | Sep | Oct | Nov | Dec |

Sandwich Tern

Sterna sandvicensis
40 cm

Another fairly common winter visitor, with occasional non-breeding birds staying over summer. May be seen in mixed flocks of terns at the water's edge on the beaches around Qatar.

The Sandwich Tern is the same size as the Lesser Crested Tern (p 213) and Gull-billed Tern (p 208) with which it often associates. It has a long, slender black bill with a yellow tip and this is the best identification mark. The conspicuous shaggy black cap is often smaller and flecked with white in winter. Like some of the other terns, the legs are short and black. Careful scanning through a large flock of terns with binoculars may reveal all three species and probably a few others as well. In flight, the Sandwich Tern appears quite noticeably white, with slightly narrower wings than other terns.

| Jan | Feb | Mar | Apr | May | Jun | Jul | Aug | Sep | Oct | Nov | Dec |

Bridled Tern

Onychoprion anaethetus
37 cm

The Bridled Tern is a migrant and breeds on offshore islands. After breeding during the summer months, the birds can often be seen from the mainland at Sealine Beach Resort and Al Wakra.

This tern is easy to identify with its black cap, sooty-black uperparts and white underparts, long wings and a long, deeply-forked tail. The white forehead and black eyestripe running from the bill to the crown give the Bridled Tern its name. The slender pointed bill and the legs are black. The birds take food from the surface of the water as well as plunge-diving for fish, and will rest on surface objects such as polystyrene floats. Well after the breeding season these terns head out for the open sea and spend the winter months there without setting foot on land for several months.

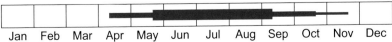

| Jan | Feb | Mar | Apr | May | Jun | Jul | Aug | Sep | Oct | Nov | Dec |

Little Tern

Sternula albifrons
22 cm

A passage migrant, the Little Tern is fractionally smaller than the similar Saunders's Tern, with a slender, yellow, black-tipped bill in summer, darkening to black in winter, and yellow legs which change to brownish-yellow in winter. The black-tipped wings and mantle are grey, and the black cap and eye stripe seen in summer reduces to a band extending from eye to eye around the back of the head in winter.

This is a small tern with a faster wing action than that of other terns, and the flight is very rapid. When plunge-diving for fish the birds poise with uplifted, vibrating wings and depressed tail acting as a rudder before closing the wings and plummeting into the sea.

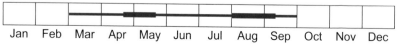

| Jan | Feb | Mar | Apr | May | Jun | Jul | Aug | Sep | Oct | Nov | Dec |

Saunders's Tern

Sternula (albifrons) saundersi
22 cm

autumn

spring

Saunders's Tern is a migrant breeder on islands off the east coast. In the loose breeding colonies individual nests are quite far apart.

This is a small bird, similar in size to the Little Tern and difficult to tell apart in the field. In breeding plumage it has a triangular white spot on the forehead. The bill is similar to that of the Little Tern: yellow with a black tip. It is very difficult to distinguish between Saunders's and Little Terns, but in flight the outermost primaries tend to show more black than those of the Little Tern, and the rump of Saunders's Tern is grey while that of the Little Tern is white. More white develops on the head outside the breeding season, and the bill darkens.

| Jan | Feb | Mar | Apr | May | Jun | Jul | Aug | Sep | Oct | Nov | Dec |

Whiskered Tern

Chlidonias hybrida
25 cm

spring

autumn

The Whiskered Tern is a common passage migrant. Like the White-winged Tern it frequents grey water lagoons and well-watered farmlands. For this reason both are referred to as 'marsh' terns, and they have the short, broad wings and tails typical of this group of terns.

These two terns look very similar in winter and cause identification problems. The Whiskered Tern is slightly larger and has a heavier, dark bill with a reddish tinge. The tail, like that of the White-winged Tern, is slightly forked. Both birds have red legs. The head pattern is a critical identification feature. The black eye of the Whiskered Tern is often hidden in the black mask which does not extend below the eye line. In breeding plumage from late spring the bird assumes a flush of dark grey across the breast and flanks. In addition to the grey back and wings there is a white patch on the cheeks below the eye. At this time, identification is straightforward.

| Jan | Feb | Mar | Apr | May | Jun | Jul | Aug | Sep | Oct | Nov | Dec |

White-winged Tern

Chlidonias leucopterus
24 cm

spring

autumn

The White-winged Tern, also known as the White-winged Black Tern, is a common passage migrant. Generally found over inland water, the habitats are the same as those of the Whiskered Tern. Frequently used sites are grey water lagoons, marshes and adjacent coastal areas.

The White-winged Tern is slightly smaller and more slender than the Whiskered Tern, with a shorter, rather stubby black bill, grey wings and back and a tail which is shallowly-forked, appearing almost square in juveniles. In winter the two species look very similar, but the eye of a White-winged Tern usually stands out from the black head marking, which extends to a level behind and below the eye. In flight the white rump is visible whereas the Whiskered Tern has a grey rump. In breeding plumage, the White-winged Tern lives up to its name with the lighter coloured wings contrasting with the blacker body plumage.

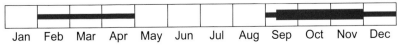

| Jan | Feb | Mar | Apr | May | Jun | Jul | Aug | Sep | Oct | Nov | Dec |

Collared Pratincole

Glareola pratincola
26 cm

The Collared Pratincole is a regular passage migrant in small numbers. With its short legs, forked tail and long pointed wings, the Collared Pratincole, although classified as a wader, resembles a tern when in flight and a plover on the ground. The call is also tern-like. However the species is easy to recognize

from the narrow black 'collar' circling from eye to eye and, in flight, the white rump. The short beak is edged with bright scarlet at the sides. If the light is good the reddish-brown underwings and the white, trailing edge to the wings are excellent field characteristics.

Collared Pratincoles tend to fly high, resembling terns or swifts, often in small flocks, in pursuit of the winged insects which are their food. They will also feed on the ground, frequenting tidal mud-flats and also farmland and semi-desert, where their plumage blends in perfectly with the sandy background.

| Jan | Feb | Mar | Apr | May | Jun | Jul | Aug | Sep | Oct | Nov | Dec |

Greater Spotted Eagle

Aquila clanga
65 cm

'fulvescens'

Classified as a 'medium-large eagle', the Greater Spotted Eagle is a passage migrant and winter visitor. It is often seen at the Abu Nakhla and Al Khor lagoons, circling over the water or perching. It has a characteristic habit of depressing the wing-tips slightly when flying and gliding.

Most of the birds seen here are juveniles, and have parallel horizontal rows of conspicuous white spots on the wings made by the pale tips of the feathers. Adults appear an overall dark brown without noticeable markings apart from a pale patch on the rump. In flight, the leading half of the underwing is almost black, and darker than the trailing half. A few Greater Spotted Eagles are pale on the upper body and are referred to as the '*fulvescens*' colour phase.

Wintering Greater Spotted Eagles are often attracted to lagoons with large numbers of wildfowl. The diet ranges from small mammals to toads, birds and insects, and it will also eat carrion.

Jan	Feb	Mar	Apr	May	Jun	Jul	Aug	Sep	Oct	Nov	Dec

Common Kingfisher

Alcedo atthis
18 cm

This small kingfisher is an infrequent but regular winter visitor to mangrove forests on the east coast and grey water lagoons - anywhere there are small fish to be caught. It will also eat small crabs on coastal mudflats.

The Common Kingfisher is a jewel of a bird. Often one just gets a glimpse of an electric-blue speck flashing past along mangrove trees or reed beds, but seen when perching it is a beauty: massive bright black-and-red bill, rufous underparts, turquoise and blue upperparts and white ear tufts. It can sit motionless for a long time on a branch overhanging the water. If a small fish is spotted below, the bird dives into the water and, if successful, brings the fish back to be consumed at the perch. It may also hover for a few seconds before plunging. The call is an unmistakable strident '*zeeee*'.

Jan	Feb	Mar	Apr	May	Jun	Jul	Aug	Sep	Oct	Nov	Dec

Pied Kingfisher

Ceryle rudis
26 cm

Pied Kingfishers are uncommon winter visitors but have been recorded on grey water lagoons such as the Al Khor and Abu Nakhla pools. The bird is easy to identify with its striking black and white plumage as it hovers above the water before plunging for fish. The white underparts have two almost complete breast bands in the male and one in the female. Sometimes two birds will be seen together, perching on a dead tree beside the water. Unlike the Common Kingfisher which has to return to a perch to consume its prey, Pied Kingfishers can deal with prey while on the wing and so can hunt over areas of water lacking perches.

| Jan | Feb | Mar | Apr | May | Jun | Jul | Aug | Sep | Oct | Nov | Dec |

Clamorous Reed Warbler   *Acrocephalus stentoreus*

17 cm

The aptly-named Clamorous Reed Warbler is a common passage migrant and migrant bre␣␣er in reed beds at wetlands such as Al Khor and Abu Nakhla. So often on approaching the reed bed one is met with a cacophony of screeching sound, but the songsters remain invisible. Eventually a bird is spotted, clinging to the top of a reed and singing vigorously. They are most likely to come out into the open in the late afternoon.

This is a uniformly brown bird lacking any conspicuous features, and closely resembling its larger relative the Great Reed Warbler. Identification characteristics include a long bill and short wings with wing-tips reaching only as far as the base of the tail on a perched bird.

| Jan | Feb | Mar | Apr | May | Jun | Jul | Aug | Sep | Oct | Nov | Dec |

Great Reed Warbler　　　*Acrocephalus arundinaceus*
18 cm

The largest of the warblers, almost as big as a Song Thrush (p 101), the Great Reed Warbler is very similar in colouring and shape to the Clamorous Reed Warbler. The bill is heavier and more pointed and the paler line through the eye slightly more pronounced. An uncommon passage migrant, it is occasionally seen at wetlands such as the Al Khor and Abu Nakhla lagoons but may also be encountered away from wetlands.

Like all warblers its main diet is insects, but it has been known to take other prey items such as beetles and small toads.

| Jan | Feb | Mar | Apr | May | Jun | Jul | Aug | Sep | Oct | Nov | Dec |

Sedge Warbler

Acrocephalus schoenobaenus
12 cm

The Sedge Warbler is a spring passage migrant, most likely to be encountered among the reed beds which surround the wetland areas at Abu Nakhla and Al Khor. A small, plump warbler, it has a flattened head with the crown streaked with black and a wide creamy stripe above the eye. The upperparts are brown with dark streaks, and the breast and belly are a pale buff.

It is mainly insectivorous, although it will also eat plant material such as small berries. Typically, Sedge Warblers feed low down in dense vegetation, picking insects from leaves and stems as they forage. When moving between perches they will also snatch insects from the air. Mostly active just after dawn and in the late afternoon.

Jan	Feb	Mar	Apr	May	Jun	Jul	Aug	Sep	Oct	Nov	Dec

Eurasian Reed Warbler   *Acrocephalus scirpaceus*
13 cm

The Eurasian Reed Warbler is an uncommon passage migrant.

A buff-coloured bird, rather slimmer and more elongated than the Sedge Warbler, the Eurasian Reed Warbler has a long flat forehead and crown, with a pale eye-ring. As its English name indicates, the bird is likely to frequent the reed beds surrounding grey water lagoons such as those at Al Khor and Abu Nakhla.

Eurasian Reed Warblers eat insects, but will also take small berries when available.

| Jan | Feb | Mar | Apr | May | Jun | Jul | Aug | Sep | Oct | Nov | Dec |

Bluethroat

Luscinia svecica
14 cm

A regular winter visitor to wetlands with reed beds such as the grey water lagoons at Abu Nakhla as well as to farmlands, parks and gardens and anywhere there is moist undergrowth.

The Bluethroat is a skulker, spending most of its time hidden away in the thick vegetation, but a brief sighting may be had as the bird suddenly appears at the edge of shrubbery or reedbeds, hopping with tail cocked and frequently flicking. The birds derive their name from their breeding plumage when they sport a bright blue bib with either a rufous or a white patch in the centre. In winter adult males visiting Qatar gradually moult to fresh spring plumage showing blue on their throats, together with surrounding bands of black, white and chestnut. The immature male and the female may not have any blue at all, but will at least have the 'necklace.' Good identification features are the rufous sides to the base of the tail.

Jan	Feb	Mar	Apr	May	Jun	Jul	Aug	Sep	Oct	Nov	Dec

Birds of the desert

Desert landscapes in Qatar are varied. But although they look different, one feature they have in common is that nowhere are birds plentiful. The number of species inhabiting desert terrain is limited, and you will find that there is usually some distance between the sightings. Nevertheless, with a bit of luck interesting birds like the Cream-coloured Courser, Eurasian Stone-curlew and several species of lark can be sighted.

Eurasian Stone-curlew

Rock Dove

The Rock Dove is a resident breeder in Qatar, inhabiting rocky jebel outcrops in the central desert and also some oases. Flocks may be seen foraging on the ground or coming to drink at permanent water supplies.

The Rock Dove is the ancestor of the domestic pigeon, and often the two can be impossible to tell apart. A flock of domestic pigeons, however, will normally include birds of different colours, some even pure white, while in a flock of wild Rock Doves all birds are the same slaty blue-grey with iridescent necks and two black bars on the wings.

Jan	Feb	Mar	Apr	May	Jun	Jul	Aug	Sep	Oct	Nov	Dec

Asian Desert Warbler

Sylvia nana
12 cm

The Asian Desert Warbler is a regular winter visitor. The preferred habitat is open desert with scattered bushes.

This little warbler with its bright orange or yellow eye and rufous tail is as easy to identify from its behaviour as from its plumage. The bird spends much time low in a bush or on the ground looking for insects as it hops around, flicking its tail. It will also eat berries when it finds them. To be warned of any predators around it often stays near a wheatear, in particular a Desert Wheatear (p 67). The wheatear sits in the top of a bush and will notice any danger. If the wheatear flies off to another bush, the Asian Desert Warbler soon follows.

| Jan | Feb | Mar | Apr | May | Jun | Jul | Aug | Sep | Oct | Nov | Dec |

Greater Hoopoe-Lark

Alaemon alaudipes
19 cm

song flight

The Greater Hoopoe-Lark is a breeding resident in all desert areas of Qatar. It is often seen while driving on desert roads as the bird takes off from the side of the road, revealing its conspicuous black and white wing pattern.

This large, slim, long-legged lark is unique. The bill is long and curved and is used to dig into the ground after insects and small lizards. The plumage is sandy-brown above with paler underparts. In early spring one may witness the spectacular song flight. The bird flies up into the air, flips over and drops, head first, vertically down while uttering a long drawn-out whistle. Just before reaching the ground it spreads its wings and lands safely.

Jan	Feb	Mar	Apr	May	Jun	Jul	Aug	Sep	Oct	Nov	Dec

Desert Lark

Ammomanes deserti
15 cm

A common breeding resident over much of the country, the Desert Lark is a rather small, nondescript, plump, greyish-brown bird without conspicuous features. The plumage can vary slightly in colour according to the habitat; some birds are darker than others. The best identification clue is the heavy, pointed bill with a black upper mandible and with yellow on the inner half of the lower mandible. In flight, the wings look reddish. Desert Larks are usually seen on the ground where they are searching for seeds. In winter, they sometimes form small flocks.

| Jan | Feb | Mar | Apr | May | Jun | Jul | Aug | Sep | Oct | Nov | Dec |

233

Greater Short-toed Lark
Calandrella brachydactyla
14 cm

The Greater Short-toed Lark is a small, rather pale bird and a fairly common passage migrant and winter visitor. Its name is misleading, as in fact its toes are not noticeably shorter than those of other larks of similar size! It frequents the semi-desert, and inland farmlands such as those at Mekainis, and also coastal salt marshes.

Though superficially similar to a Eurasian Skylark (p 105), the Greater Short-toed Lark has a rufous crown and white supercilium and lacks the vertical streaks on the breast. The strong bill is pale and the tail is dark. An excellent identification clue is a black spot on either side of the neck. During winter it is often found in flocks.

Jan	Feb	Mar	Apr	May	Jun	Jul	Aug	Sep	Oct	Nov	Dec

Lesser Short-toed Lark

Calandrella rufescens
13 cm

A uncommon passage migrant and winter visitor, this small lark closely resembles its relative, the Greater Short-toed Lark, but lacks the dark spot on the neck and the white supercilium. The head is more rounded in shape and the bill more stubby. Dark streaks on the breast help in identification.

Unlike the Greater Short-toed Lark which is also found on cultivated land, this bird prefers arid, open country and is more likely to be encountered in the true desert.

Jan	Feb	Mar	Apr	May	Jun	Jul	Aug	Sep	Oct	Nov	Dec

Cream-coloured Courser

Cursorius cursor
26 cm

The Cream-coloured Courser is a passage migrant, winter visitor and scarce resident breeder. Although classed as waders, they inhabit dry open semi-desert, where they hunt their insect prey by running fast.

Except for the bold head pattern, this species with its uniformly beige colours blends in perfectly with its arid surroundings. When standing it has an erect posture; the long legs are pale. When remaining still it can be difficult to see. The black and white stripes through and above each eye meet at the back of the neck, and the bill is slightly downcurved. Whether looking for food or to escape danger, the birds prefer to run; only as a last resort will they take to the wing. In flight the whole outer half of each wing is black.

Jan	Feb	Mar	Apr	May	Jun	Jul	Aug	Sep	Oct	Nov	Dec

Eurasian Stone-curlew

Other name: Eurasian Thick-knee

Burhinus oedicnemus
38 cm

These birds have large yellow eyes, a strong yellow and black bill and brown streaked and mottled plumage. In flight, black and white wing markings are noticeable. Its scientific name refers to the thickened, prominent joints on the long, yellowish-green legs. This joint is actually the heel, as the knee in all birds is hidden in the belly feathers.

Although classed as a wader, it prefers the dry habitat of the open desert. The large eyes are an indication that it is largely nocturnal in activity. Its calls at night are reminiscent of those of curlews. If disturbed during the day, Eurasian Stone-curlews remain motionless, relying on their plumage for camouflage and only running off at the last moment. If pressed they take to the wing to fly low over the ground with fast, shallow wingbeats.

Jan	Feb	Mar	Apr	May	Jun	Jul	Aug	Sep	Oct	Nov	Dec

237

Pharaoh Eagle Owl

Bubo ascalaphus
50 cm

The Pharaoh Eagle Owl is the largest species of owl found in Qatar. It is an uncommon winter visitor and an occasional breeding resident in recent years. Its size, prominent ear tufts and large, bright orange eyes make this majestic owl instantly recognisable.

Pharaoh Eagle Owls are birds of the wilderness and although normally nocturnal may sometimes be surprised at a roosting site during the day. Their food generally consists of small desert rodents and birds, and invertebrates such as beetles and scorpions, but Pharaoh Eagle Owls have been known to take prey as large as foxes and hares.

Jan	Feb	Mar	Apr	May	Jun	Jul	Aug	Sep	Oct	Nov	Dec

Long-legged Buzzard

Buteo rufinus
60 cm

Long-legged Buzzards are frequent winter visitors, preferring the open desert and semi-desert to wetland and cultivated areas. The birds have a distinctive appearance, with very dark brown mantle and wings having a faint rufous tinge, reddish-orange underparts and a pale cream breast and head with few or no markings. In flight the black primary feathers are visible. The tail is pale rufous.

These buzzards feed mainly on small rodents such as gerbils and jerds, although they will also take small reptiles, birds and insects.

| Jan | Feb | Mar | Apr | May | Jun | Jul | Aug | Sep | Oct | Nov | Dec |

Common Ostrich

Struthio camelus
230 cm

male

female

A flock of free-ranging Common Ostriches has been introduced to the area of the old oasis at Ras Abrouq, beside which stands a recently built film set. These birds are from Africa and are not the subspecies, *Struthio camelus syriacus*, the Arabian Ostrich, which originally inhabited the deserts of southern Arabia and became extinct in the 1920s. Male Common Ostriches can become very aggressive during the breeding season, the winter and spring months, and should not be approached on foot.

| Jan | Feb | Mar | Apr | May | Jun | Jul | Aug | Sep | Oct | Nov | Dec |

Eurasian Hoopoe

Index of scientific names

Laughing Dove

Index of English names

Against each species are two small check boxes. Use them to tick off a species when you have seen it and thus keep a running total of the number of birds you have recorded. Two people can use the list with one column of boxes used by each person. A friendly competition can emerge.

White Wagtail

About the authors

Hanne & Jens Eriksen have lived in Oman and the UAE for the past 25 years and have traveled extensively in Arabia, the Middle East and all seven continents to study and photograph birds. They are authors or co-authors of seven books on birds including *Birdwatching guide to Oman* and *Common Birds in Oman*. They have won several photo competitions and more than 10,000 of their pictures have been published worldwide.

Frances Gillespie is a free-lance writer and journalist who has lived in Qatar for more than 25 years. She is the author or co-author of a number of books on the country, including *Discovering Qatar* published in 2006. Frances lists bird-watching as just one of her hobbies, which include exploring the off-road regions to study and record the fauna and flora, and the archaeology of Qatar.